SHEPHERD'S NOTES

Shepherd's Notes Titles Available

SHEPHERD'S NOTES COMMENTARY SERIES

Old Testament

0-80549-028-0	Genesis	0-80549-341-7	Psalms 101-150
0-80549-056-6	Exodus	0-80549-016-7	Proverbs
0-80549-069-8	Leviticus & Numbers	0-80549-059-0	Ecclesiastes, Song of
0-80549-027-2	Deuteronomy		Solomon
0-80549-058-2	Joshua & Judges	0-80549-197-X	Isaiah
0-80549-057-4	Ruth & Esther	0-80549-070-1	Jeremiah-
0-80549-063-9	1 & 2 Samuel		Lamentations
0-80549-007-8	1 & 2 Kings	0-80549-078-7	Ezekiel
0-80549-064-7	1 & 2 Chronicles	0-80549-015-9	Daniel
0-80549-194-5	Ezra, Nehemiah	0-80549-326-3	Hosea-Obadiah
0-80549-006-X	Job	0-80549-334-4	Jonah-Zephaniah
0-80549-339-5	Psalms 1-50	0-80549-065-5	Haggai-Malachi
0-80549-340-9	Psalms 51-100		

New Testament

1-55819-688-9	Matthew	1-55819-689-7	Philippians,
0-80549-071-X	Mark		Colossians, &
0-80549-004-3	Luke		Philemon
1-55819-693-5	John	0-80549-000-0	1 & 2 Thessalonians
1-55819-691-9	Acts	1-55819-692-7	1 & 2 Timothy, Titus
0-80549-005-1	Romans	0-80549-336-0	Hebrews
0-80549-325-5	1 Corinthians	0-80549-018-3	James
0-80549-335-2	2 Corinthians	0-80549-019-1	1 & 2 Peter & Jude
1-55819-690-0	Galatians	0-80549-214-3	1, 2 & 3 John
0-80549-327-1	Ephesians	0-80549-017-5	Revelation

SHEPHERD'S NOTES CHRISTIAN CLASSICS

0-80549-347-6	Mere Christianity-C.S.Lewis	0-80549-394-8	Miracles-C.S.Lewis
0-80549-353-0	The Problem of Pain/ A Grief Observed-C.S.Lewis	0-80549-196-1	Lectures to My Students-Charles Haddon Spurgeon
0-80549-199-6	The Confessions-Augustine	0-80549-220-8	The Writings of Justin Martyr
0-80549-200-3	Calvin's Institutes	0-80549-345-X	The City of God

SHEPHERD'S NOTES-BIBLE SUMMARY SERIES

0-80549-377-8	Old Testament	0-80549-385-9	Life & Letters of Paul
0-80549-378-6	New Testament	0-80549-376-X	Manners & Customs of Bible Times
0-80549-384-0	Life & Teachings of Jesus	0-80549-380-8	Basic Christian Beliefs

SHEPHERD'S NOTES

When you need a guide through the Scriptures

I, II Timothy / Titus

BROADMAN
&HOLMAN
PUBLISHERS

Nashville, Tennessee

Shepherd's Notes, *1, 2 Timothy and Titus*
© 1997 Broadman & Holman Publishers, Nashville, Tennessee
All rights reserved
Printed in the United States of America

ISBN# 1–55819–692–7

Dewey Decimal Classification: 227.83
Subject Headings: BIBLE. N.T. TIMOTHY
BIBLE. N.T. TITUS

Library of Congress Card Catalog Number: 97–25907

Other translation used:

The Pastoral Epistles in the Greek New Testament for the English Reader by Kenneth S. Wuest, © 1952 Wm. B. Eerdmans Publishing Co., Grand Rapids, Mich.

Library of Congress Cataloging-in-Publication Data

1, 2 Timothy, Titus / Dana Gould, editor.
    p. cm. (Shepherd's Notes)
Includes bibliographical references.
ISBN 1–55819–692–7
    1. Bible. N.T. Pastoral Epistles—Study and teaching.
  I. Gould, Dana, 1951–.   II. Title: First, Second Timothy, Titus. III. Series
BS2735.5.A16   1998
227.83'06—DC21

97–25907
CIP

6 7 8   06
R

CONTENTS

Foreword vi

How to Use This Book vii

Introduction   1

First Timothy   9

1 Timothy 1   9

1 Timothy 2 14

1 Timothy 3 18

1 Timothy 4 26

1 Timothy 5 29

1 Timothy 6 34

Second Timothy 42

2 Timothy 1 42

2 Timothy 2 48

2 Timothy 3 55

2 Timothy 4 59

Titus 66

Titus 1 66

Titus 2 72

Titus 3 78

Reference Sources Used 85

FOREWORD

Dear Reader:

Shepherd's Notes are designed to give you a quick, step-by-step overview of every book of the Bible. They are not meant to be a substitute for the biblical text; rather, they are study guides intended to help you explore the wisdom of Scripture in personal or group study and to apply that wisdom successfully in your own life.

Shepherd's Notes guide you through both the main themes of each book of the Bible and illuminate fascinating details through appropriate commentary and reference notes. Historical and cultural background information brings the Bible into sharper focus.

Six different icons, used throughout the series, call your attention to historical-cultural information, Old Testament and New Testament references, word pictures, unit summaries, and personal application for everyday life.

Whether you are a novice or a veteran at Bible study, I believe you will find *Shepherd's Notes* a resource that will take you to a new level in your mining and applying the riches of Scripture.

In Him,

David R. Shepherd
Editor-in-Chief

DESIGNED FOR THE BUSY USER

Shepherd's Notes for 1 and 2 Timothy and Titus is designed to provide an easy-to use tool for getting a quick handle on these Bible books important features, and for gaining an understanding of the message of the Pastoral Epistles. Information available in more difficult-to-use reference works has been incorporated into the *Shepherd's Notes* format. This brings you the benefits of many more advanced and expensive works packed into one small volume.

Shepherd's Notes are for laymen, pastors, teachers, small group leaders and participants, as well as the classroom student. Enrich your personal study or quiet time. Shorten your class or small group preparation time as you gain valuable insights into the truths of God's Word that you can pass along to your students or group members.

DESIGNED FOR QUICK ACCESS

Bible students with time constraints will especially appreciate the timesaving features built into the *Shepherd's Notes*. All features are intended to aid a quick and concise encounter with the heart of the message of the Pastoral Epistles.

Concise Commentary. 1 and 2 Timothy and Titus are filled with characters, places, events, and instruction to believers. Short sections provide quick "snapshots" of the apostle Paul's narratives and arguments, highlighting important points and other information.

Outlined Text. A comprehensive outline covers the entire text of 1 and 2 Timothy and Titus. This is a valuable feature for following the narrative's flow, allowing for a quick, easy way to locate a particular passage.

Shepherd's Notes. These summary statements appear at the close of every key section of the narrative. While functioning in part as a quick summary, they also deliver the essence of the message presented in the sections which they cover.

Icons. Various icons in the margin highlight recurring themes in the Pastoral Epistles and aid in selective searching or tracing of those themes.

Sidebars and Charts. These specially selected features provide additional background information to your study or preparation. These include definitions as well as cultural, historical, and biblical insights.

Maps. These are placed at appropriate places in the book to aid your understanding and study of a text or passage.

Questions to Guide Your Study. These thought-provoking questions and discussion starters are designed to encourage interaction with the truth and principles of God's Word.

DESIGNED TO WORK FOR YOU

Personal Study. Using the Shepherd's Notes with a passage of Scripture can enlighten your study and take it to a new level. At your fingertips is information that would require searching several volumes to find. In addition, many points of application occur throughout the volume, contributing to your personal growth.

Teaching. Outlines frame the text of 1 and 2 Timothy and Titus, providing a logical presentation of the message. Capsule thoughts designated "Shepherd's Notes" provide summary statements for presenting the essence of key points and events. Application icons point out personal application of the message of 1 and 2 Timothy and Titus. Historical Context and Cultural Context icons indicate where background information is supplied.

Group Study. These *Shepherd's Notes* can be an excellent companion volume to use for gaining a quick but accurate understanding of the message of a Bible book. Each group member can benefit by having his or her own copy. The *Note's* format accommodates the study of or the tracing of themes throughout the Pastoral Epistles. Leaders may use its flexible features to prepare for group sessions or use them during group sessions. Guiding Questions can spark discussion of the key points and truths of the message of 1 and 2 Timothy and Titus.

LIST OF MARGIN ICONS USED IN 1 AND 2 TIMOTHY AND TITUS

Shepherd's Notes. Placed at the end of each section, a capsule statement that provides the reader with the essence of the message of that section.

Old Testament Reference. Used when the writer refers to Old Testament Scripture passages that are related or have a bearing on the passage's understanding or interpretation.

New Testament Reference. Used when the writer refers to New Testament passages that are related to or have a bearing on the passage's understanding or interpretation.

Historical Background. To indicate historical, cultural, geographical, or biographical information that sheds light on the understanding or interpretation of a passage.

Personal Application. Used when the text provides a personal or universal application of truth.

Word Picture. Indicates that the meaning of a specific word or phrase is illustrated so as to shed light on it.

INTRODUCTION

This introduction covers the Books of 1 and 2 Timothy and Titus. This group of letters is known as the Pastoral Epistles or the Pastoral Letters. These letters were written near the end of Paul's life to guide his two younger associates.

AUTHOR

The apostle Paul is credited with writing the Pastoral Epistles. Each of the Pastoral Letters includes Paul as its writer. Although some scholars have raised questions about stylistic contrasts between these letters and other Pauline Epistles, it is unnecessary to reject Paul as author on that basis. After all considerations, much weight of evidence exists to support direct or indirect authorship of Paul for these three letters.

PLACE AND DATE OF WRITING

First Timothy. The place of this epistle's origination is uncertain, but somewhere in Macedonia seems to be the most likely location, a conclusion drawn from 1:3. The time of writing is difficult to determine, but probably some time between A.D. 63 and 67 is a good possibility.

Second Timothy. This letter supports Rome as the place of imprisonment (1:16–17). The most likely date for 2 Timothy is between A.D. 63 and 67.

Titus. The place of origin was somewhere in Macedonia. Paul wrote Titus before 2 Timothy, and perhaps before 1 Timothy. For Paul to have written the letter, the date most likely would be the same as for 1 and 2 Timothy, A.D. 63–67.

OCCASION AND PURPOSE OF WRITING OF THE PASTORALS

Occasion. The Pastoral Letters were written to deal with the false teaching that was negatively impacting the young churches. The churches were apparently in more danger from internal threats than from external persecution. Paul urged his apostolic associates to counter the internal danger with sound teaching, by providing an example of godly living, and by organizing and training leaders for the congregations.

Purpose. These letters address the need for pastoral oversight in the churches. They focus on church organization, the importance of apostolic doctrine, and the refutation of false doctrine. First Timothy and Titus carefully describe the qualifications of Christian leaders

AUDIENCE
First Timothy. Timothy was the primary reader of this epistle, but certainly he shared the contents with the church. He was a trusted friend and fellow-laborer to Paul in the Gentile mission.

Second Timothy. The letter names Timothy as the recipient. Paul's worst fears, hinted at in 1 Timothy, have been realized, and he is once again in prison (4:8, 16).

Titus. Titus is the recipient. He had leadership responsibilities for the church at Crete. A Gentile, Titus was an important fellow worker with Paul. The instructions are general enough in Titus so as to be read by or to the entire church.

MAJOR THEMES IN THE PASTORAL LETTERS
The Gospel. In all three of the Pastoral Epistles a concern for the truth of the gospel is a powerful influence. Paul uses both the courtroom image of justification and the social image of redemption to describe the results of responding to the gospel. Paul presents faith as the proper response to the gospel and emphasizes that godly living must be a result of this faith response.

Church Government. Paul pictures the church in the Pastoral Epistles as a united family ministering to its constituency and organized for service. The church is the family of God, and believers are brothers and sisters. Paul charged the church with a responsibility to the poor and to serve as a foundation of doctrinal and ethical truth. Leaders of the church were known as overseers or elders, and they were assisted by deacons. Women also filled a special position of service in the church.

Heresy. In the second century, Christianity became involved in a fierce struggle with a heretical movement known as Gnosticism. This false teaching denied the Resurrection of Christ, vacillated between moral license and rigid asceticism, and insisted that sinful human beings could not enjoy fellowship and full contact with the transcendent God. The heresy Paul describes in the Pastoral Epistles was characterized by an interest in Jewish law (1 Tim. 1:6–7) and showed the influence of "those of the circumcision group" (Titus 1:10).

Salvation. The Pastoral Epistles recognize the universal problem of sin and God's desire to redeem humanity from sin's power and penalty. Both God and Jesus Christ are referred to as "Savior" throughout the Pastorals. Paul boldly asserts that "Christ Jesus came into the world to save sinners" (1 Tim. 1:15) Salvation is God's work alone, promised by God before the beginning of time, and historically realized at His "appointed season" (Titus 1:3). Believers are referred to as Christ's elect, as redeemed through Christ's self-sacrifice, and can be described as "saved," "reborn," "renewed," and "justified" (Titus 3:5–7).

The Trinity. Paul describes God the Father by reference to His attributes and His actions. He portrays God as living and as observing the moral actions of His creatures. Paul refers to God as eternal, immortal, invisible, and as the only God. He reflects monotheism by his reference to God as one. The majesty of God is such that He is unapproachable, deserving of blessing and thanksgiving from His creatures. God is also faithful and truthful to His promises, merciful in salvation, and generous in giving the Holy Spirit. Paul also describes God as Creator and the Bestower of life. He is the sovereign ruler who has condescended to reveal Himself in Scripture. The course of all history is in His hands.

THEOLOGICAL SIGNIFICANCE OF THE PASTORAL LETTERS

First Timothy. The letter to Timothy develops a theology of the church. The church needs organization to do its work effectively. Church leaders give guidance and enablement for the Christian community to carry out its service. The church is to be a pillar and bulwark, a custodian of the truth. The church must always strive to avoid heresy and to teach the truths of the gospel to succeeding generations.

Second Timothy. This second letter to Timothy teaches us about the importance of our theological heritage (1:14). Paul had much to say about what God has done in Christ, our Savior. Jesus Christ has been revealed, has destroyed death, and has given us life and immortality (1:8–10). The foundation of the Christian life is what God has already done for us in Christ. We should live boldly, for we have received a "spirit of power, of love and of self-discipline" (1:7). These truths about the gospel and Christian living are available to us in God's inspired Scripture (3:15–17). Now we, like Timothy, should pass on these truths to faithful men and women who can also teach others (2:2).

Titus. Like the other Pastoral Letters, Paul's Letter to Titus focuses on keeping the faith and refuting heresy. Especially significant, considering the nature of the Cretan heresy, are the repeated emphases on doctrinal fidelity (2:11–14; 3:4–7) and faithful living (1:16; 2:7, 14; 3:1, 8, 14). The letter makes it plain that the Christian life is grounded in the grace of God (2:11–14). Believers must recognize this truth and rebuke heresy and avoid legalism (1:10–16). This can be done only by grace—grace that saves, grace that teaches, grace that strengthens, and grace that enables. In so doing, we can see the relationship between doctrine and practice.

THE VALUE OF THE PASTORAL LETTERS FOR TODAY

The Pastorals provide insight. They help us in dealing with contemporary problems of heresy, divisiveness, and leadership difficulties.

They are not a collection of rigid rules for church organization, but guidelines which provide direction for facing problems and church needs.

The Pastorals are realistic. They present the churches Paul founded with all their needs, weaknesses, and shortcomings (1 Tim. 4:1–3). However, they also present the mighty power of God as a prescription for human failure (1 Tim. 1:17), and they show this divine power at work in the lives of people (1 Tim. 1:12–17).

The Pastorals provide encouragement. In spite of the likelihood that Paul was facing death as he wrote 2 Timothy, he remained steadfastly optimistic (2 Tim. 4:6–8), He was lonely, but he was vigilant, irrepressibly a preacher, and confident in the Lord. The Pastorals provide a picture of the early church as it faced error, greed, and moral corruption. In spite of these shortcomings, there is a clear sign of anticipated victory and hopeful moral restitution. Churches today need a heavy dose of such realism and encouragement.

One additional feature of significance in the Pastorals is their influence on hymnody. Some of the better-known hymns based on the Pastorals include "Immortal, Invisible, God Only Wise (1 Tim. 1:17), "Fight the Good Fight" (1 Tim. 6:12), and "I Know Whom I Have Believed" (2 Tim. 1:12).

OUTLINES OF THE PASTORAL LETTERS

Basic Outline of 1 Timothy:
  I. Introduction (1:1–2)
  II. Warning Against False Teachers (1:3–20)
  III. Guidelines for Church Worship (2:1–15)
  IV. Instructions for Church Leadership (3:1–13)
  V. Maintaining the Truth (3:14–4:16)
  VI. Miscellaneous Instructions for the Church (5:1–6:10)
  VII. Personal Charge to Timothy (6:11–21)

Basic Outline of Second Timothy:
 I. Introduction (1:1–7)
 II. Suffering and the Gospel (1:8–18)
 III. Encouragement to Faithfulness (2:1–13)
 IV. Contrasts in the Church (2:14–26)
 V. Godlessness in the Last Days (3:1–9)
 VI. Final Advice to Timothy (3:10–4:18)
 VII. Final Greetings (4:19–22)

Basic Outline of Titus:
 I. Introduction (1:1–4)
 II. The Appointment of Elders (1:5–9)
 III. The Rebuke of False Teachers (1:10–16)
 IV. The Different Groups in the Church (2:1–15)
 V. The Responsibility of Christian Living (3:1–11)
 VI. Personal Concluding Requests (3:12–15)

GUIDING QUESTIONS

 1. What issues prompted Paul's letters to Timothy and Titus?
 2. What were Paul's circumstances at the time of his writing of the Pastoral Epistles?
 3. Examine the major themes in the Pastorals. How are these relevant to the mission and work of the church today?
 4. What is the value of the Pastoral Letters to the church today?

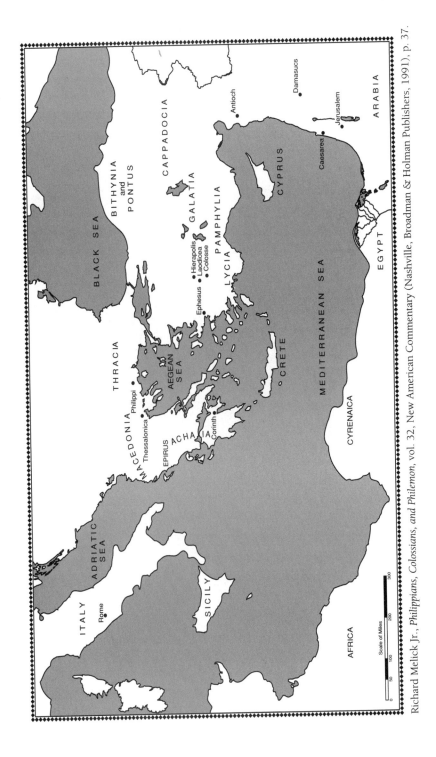

Richard Melick Jr., *Philippians, Colossians, and Philemon*, vol. 32, New American Commentary (Nashville, Broadman & Holman Publishers, 1991), p. 37.

1 TIMOTHY 1

Timothy

SALUTATION (1:1–2)

In the address of his letters, Paul follows the form of first-century letter writing. Three of the elements of that form give structure to the opening of 1 Timothy. They are: the name of the writer, the name of the recipient, and a greeting.

Author (v. 1)

The letter's author is Paul the apostle. "Paul" was the Gentile name of the great missionary statesman and was used to designate the writer in each of the thirteen Pauline Epistles.

Recipient (v. 2a)

Timothy is the recipient of this letter. He was one of the close associates of Paul in his missionary labors. In fact, Timothy accompanied Paul on his second and third missionary journeys. The biblical portrait of Timothy is that of a young man, somewhat retiring and perhaps shy. Paul urged his young disciple to stand firm for the gospel against menacing opponents and circumstances.

Greeting (v. 2b)

Outside of this letter among Paul's writings, only 2 Tim. 1:2 employs a threefold greeting of "grace, mercy, and peace." As Paul's special representative in a difficult situation, Timothy had great need for an abundant supply of all three qualities. Detailed, these qualities mean:

Grace. This describes the gracious goodness that God offers to undeserving sinners.

Timothy's name means "honoring God." When Timothy was a child, his mother Eunice and his grandmother Lois taught him the Scriptures (2 Tim. 1:5; 3:15). A native of Lystra, he may have been converted on Paul's first missionary journey (Acts 14:6–23). Paul referred to Timothy as his child in the faith (1 Cor. 4:17; 1 Tim. 1:2; 2 Tim. 1:2). This probably means that Paul was instrumental in Timothy's conversion.

When Paul came to Lystra on his second journey, Timothy was a disciple who was well-respected by the believers (Acts 16:1–2). Paul asked Timothy to accompany him. Timothy's father was a Greek, and Timothy had not been circumcised. Because they would be ministering to many Jews and because Timothy's mother was Jewish, Paul had Timothy circumcised (Acts 16:3).

Timothy not only accompanied Paul but also was sent on many crucial missions by Paul. For example, when Paul was unable to go to Corinth, he sent Timothy to represent Paul and his teachings (1 Cor. 4:17). Later, when Paul was in prison, he sent Timothy to Philippi (Phil. 2:19). Paul felt that no one had more compassion and commitment than Timothy (vv. 20–22). So close were Paul and Timothy that both names are listed as the authors on six of Paul's letters.

"Meaningless talk"

This phrase is one word in New Testament Greek, a compound word composed of two words: *vain* and to *speak*. In addition to the NIV's rendering, "meaningless talk," this word is variously translated "empty prattle" (TDNT) "vain talking" (A. T. Robertson), "talking idly" (Vines), and "talking foolishness" (NLT). In 1 Timothy 1:6 it is used of those who have turned their backs on a pure heart, a good conscience, and a sincere faith.

Mercy. This is God's help offered to the discouraged and stumbling (Heb. 4:16).

Peace. This describes a state of salvation that results from the grace and mercy of God.

THE EXPLANATION OF THE TASK TO TIMOTHY (1:3–20)

Paul wasted no time in explaining the aim and purpose of the letter. He directed Timothy to remain in Ephesus so that he could warn church leaders not to involve themselves in the spread of false belief and practice.

Paul charged Timothy to maintain his commitment and obedience to the Lord in order to avoid the decline of commitment that had overtaken Hymenaeus and Alexander.

PREVENT THE SPREAD OF FALSE TEACHING (1:3–11)

Timothy was to order certain men in Ephesus to stop spreading speculative ideas that promoted controversy rather than the work of God.

Content of the Warning (vv. 3–4)

Paul warns against "myths and endless genealogies" (v. 4). Interpreters see these stories as either fictitious distortions of the Old Testament or Gnostic myths about creation. Paul opposes these myths because they get God's people sidetracked in speculation and argument rather than focusing on the work of proclaiming the gospel and nurturing believers in the Christian life.

Goal of the Warning (vv. 5–7)

The purpose of Christian instruction or preaching is to lead people to grow in both their love of God and other human beings. Mature love flows from hearts that are being purified, consciences which are cleansed, and faith that is without pretense.

By describing the false teachers as "teachers of the law," Paul pictures them as aspiring to be like Jewish rabbis and spinning out sterile interpretations of Old Testament stories and regulations. These "teachers" pretended to be wise sages, but they were really talking about matters they didn't begin to understand.

Reason for the Warning (vv. 8–11)

Paul's reason for warning against the false teachers at Ephesus was that they had misunderstood the intent and the use of God's law. They were using the law *unlawfully* and perverting its true function in God's plan.

What is the right use of the Law? From Paul's other writings, we see that the primary function of the Law is to make us aware of sin and of our need for Christ's forgiveness.

In his statement that the Law "is made not for the righteous," Paul is saying that committed believers do not need the Law to propel them to holy living. Their new heart takes pleasure in God's Law and they are open to the promptings of the Holy Spirit which leads them to act in ways that fulfill God's Law (Gal. 5:22–24).

"Christian love"

The special kind of love Paul speaks of here is known as *agape* love. Paul's understanding and discussion of love make it a central theme, and his use of the noun *agape* makes the term almost a technical word. Prior to Paul, in fact, the Greek term *agape* was little used. Instead of using a word for love already filled with meaning, Paul took the seldom-used term and filled it with Christian meaning.

Christian love is not simply an emotion that arises because of the character of the one loved. It is not due to the loving quality of the lover. It is a relationship of self giving that results from God's activity in Christ. The source of Christian love is God (Rom. 5:8), and the believer's response of faith makes love a human possibility (Rom. 5:5).

■ *Paul warns against the false doctrines per-*
■ *meating Ephesus. His statements are blunt*
■ *and incisive. He accuses the heretics of not*
■ *properly understanding and using the Law.*

TO PREACH THE GOSPEL (1:12–17)

In this passage, Paul explains the unlimited power of the gospel. These verses are a sort of

At the close of his second missionary journey, Paul left Greece, taking Pricilla and Aquila with him. They stopped at Ephesus. The Christians there urged Paul to stay but he declined. He left Aquila, Pricilla, and perhaps Timothy. Paul returned to Ephesus on his third missionary journey and spent three years there (Acts 20:31).

"Trustworthy"

This passage introduces the first of five sections in the Pastoral Epistles that contain the term *trustworthy*. All five passages contain the formula statement, "Here is a trustworthy saying." This term *trustworthy* means "reliable, worthy of full confidence." Each occurrence marks an article of belief that is worthy of acceptance and deeply cherished by all believers. Some scholars affirm that each saying contains an application to the present of some aspect or feature of salvation (M. Dibelius and H Conzelmann, *The Pastoral Epistles* [Philadelphia: Fortress, 1972], p. 29).

parenthesis that is an outburst of praise for the grace of God.

Thanksgiving to God (vv. 12–14)
Paul expresses three attitudes that are characteristic of his view of ministry:

1. Christ Himself is the source of Paul's strength. Paul doesn't take credit for any of his accomplishments.
2. Being a servant of Jesus Christ is a privilege beyond comprehension. He considers it a blessing he did not deserve.
3. When Christ calls a person into His service, this implies trust. Paul felt great responsibility for living up to that trust.

Statement of the Gospel (vv. 15–16)
In this verse, Paul succinctly summarizes the gospel. In contrast to the complex arguments and speculations of false teachers, Paul states the gospel in nine words: Christ Jesus came into the world to save sinners.

He goes on to say that he himself was the worst case—as if to say, *He saved me; therefore He can save anyone.*

The "Trustworthy Sayings" Formula in the Pastoral Epistles

"HERE IS A TRUSTWORTHY SAYING . . ."
1 Timothy 1:15
1 Timothy 3:1
1 Timothy 4:9
2 Timothy 2:11
Titus 3:8

Doxology (v. 17)

As Paul contemplates the incredible redeeming grace of God, what had begun as a thanksgiving now concludes with a doxology of divine praise. He ascribes these characteristics to God:

1. "The King eternal." His rule is universal and eternal.
2. "Immortal." He is immune from decay and corruption.
3. "Invisible." But believers can view the splendid glory of God residing in the person of Jesus (2 Cor. 4:6; John 1:14).

- *Paul summarizes the gospel in clear language, presenting himself as exhibit A of what the gospel can do in the life of a sinner.*
- *The very thought of this causes him to thank God for what He has done and to praise Him for Who He is.*

AN ENCOURAGING REMINDER (1:18–20)

Paul is about to instruct Timothy regarding the situation in Ephesus. He prefaces his instruction with three reminders—two positive and one negative.

First, Timothy will find strength for fighting the good fight by remembering the prophecies made at the time he was set apart for Christian ministry.

Second, two characteristics that will contribute to Timothy's strength as God's man in Ephesus are faith and a good conscience.

Third, Paul reminds Timothy of what happens when Christians jettison faith and a good

"Delivered unto Satan"

Many scholars believe this means that the church withdrew fellowship from these men in order to enable them to realize the gravity of what they were doing. We see an instance of this at Corinth (1 Cor. 5: 1–5; 2 Cor. 4: 4–8).

conscience. Hymenaeus and Alexander were "wreckers of faith" in Ephesus. As a result, Paul delivered them to Satan to teach them not to blaspheme.

■ *Paul takes a moment to encourage Timothy,*
■ *reminding him of truths that would equip*
■ *him for his leadership role in Ephesus.*

GUIDING QUESTIONS

1. Describe Paul's warning to Timothy about false teachers. What was Paul's greatest concern?
2. What is *agape*, or Christian, love? Contrast it with the attitudes of those false teachers.
3. What was Paul's view of ministry? How applicable is his view for those in ministry today?
4. What is the point of the "trustworthy sayings" in the Pastoral Epistles? What do some scholars think about these?

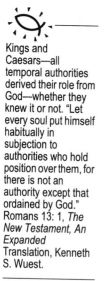

Kings and Caesars—all temporal authorities derived their role from God—whether they knew it or not. "Let every soul put himself habitually in subjection to authorities who hold position over them, for there is not an authority except that ordained by God." Romans 13: 1, *The New Testament, An Expanded Translation*, Kenneth S. Wuest.

1 TIMOTHY 2

Paul turns from warnings about false teachers to the subject of worship and how it should be conducted.

THE SCOPE OF PUBLIC PRAYER (2:1–7)

The Objects and Content of Prayer (vv. 1–2)
Objects of prayer. The church has a role as intercessor, not only for those in its fellowship, but also for everybody outside its community. Paul specifically mentions kings—those who have authority over temporal matters.

Content of Prayer. Paul lists four words for prayer: requests, prayers, intercession, and thanksgiving.

Four Words for Prayer in 1 Timothy 2:1

WORD	ITS USE
Requests	Used of petitions to God based on a sense of deep spiritual need
Prayers	For all kinds of prayers to God including the general requests or specific petitions
Intercession	Used of Christ's prayers for believers
Thanksgiving	Adds gratitude as a motivation for asking

Paul probably did not intend any sharp distinction between these words. Perhaps he was collecting synonyms that effectively communicate the importance of prayer.

The Goal of Prayer (vv. 3–4)

The goal of the prayers Paul urges is that all people be saved. This is to include all human beings, without distinctions of race or social standing. That God desires ("wants") the salvation of all people does not guarantee that all will be saved. God will not override the reluctance or opposition of individuals bent upon pursuing their own way in defiance of God.

The will of God does not function as a ruthless bulldozer, crushing and forcing into obedience any who resist it. God urges us to repentance with His goodness rather than coercing us toward the truth with His power. To come to the "knowledge of the truth" is a synonym for conversion.

"Ransom"

This word is made up of two words, one of which has the primary meaning of freeing slaves and prisoners. The second word means "on behalf of" or "instead of." It suggests substitution. In the world of slaves and prisoners, money is paid and a slave is freed. The owner of the slave is satisfied with the payment.

The Goal of Prayer (vv. 5–7)

As he has done earlier in the letter, Paul simply states foundational truths which stand in sharp contrast to complicated speculations.

1. There is one God.
2. There is a single mediator between God and humankind.
3. Christ's death was a ransom.

Paul himself was an example of God's universal purpose. By divine appointment he was a "herald and an apostle." Through him, God was reaching out to the pagan world which his fellow Jews had excluded from the covenant community.

The goal of the prayers Paul urges is that all people be saved. Jesus' death is the price paid for the release of humankind from captivity to sin. Although Christ's death has the potential to save all people, it is effective only with those who come to Christ in faith and repentance.

INSTRUCTIONS FOR WORSHIP (2:8–15)

Paul turns to instructions regarding public worship.

An Appeal to the Men (v. 8)

In the early church, the place of worship was usually the home of some believer. By implication, the men were to do the public praying. A common Jewish posture in prayer was evidently widely adopted by early Christians. While they stood, they looked upward toward heaven, lifting their arms with the palms turned upward. This may have symbolized the expectation of receiving God's blessings in answer to their petitions. Of course, no specific posture in prayer is sacred. Various postures are found in Scripture.

Paul's primary point in this passage, however, is not the posture of prayer but the attitude which the men were to bring to prayer. They were to pray "without anger or disputing."

An Appeal to Women (vv. 9–15)

The moral behavior of the women (vv. 9–10). Paul's first point has to do with the way women were to dress when they attended the public worship of the church. Modesty is to be the governing principle. The worship service is not the place for a fashion show. He urges the women to produce good works instead of devoting attention to their physical appearance. There should be a relationship between behavior and belief, between deeds and profession.

The church activity of the women (vv. 11–12). By late twentieth-century standards, Paul is far from politically correct, but he is clear that women are to focus on being learners rather than teachers in the context of a congregation of believers.

An explanation of Paul's appeal (vv. 13–14). Drawing on the account of the Creation in Genesis 2, Paul argues that Adam was chronologically prior to Eve. This chronological priority becomes the support of Paul's command that the women were to show a spirit of attentiveness to learning and were to avoid an attempt at dominating men. Paul apparently feels that the spiritual equality of both men and women in Christ (Gal. 3:28) does not negate differences in role that are part of God's creative design.

Moreover, Paul relates his prohibition to the history of the Fall in Genesis 3. Eve was deceived

"So when you offer your gift to God at the altar, and you remember that your brother has something against you, leave your gift there at the altar. Go and make peace with him. Then come and offer your gift."
Matthew 5: 23–24,
NCV

by the serpent and so fell into sin. In describing Adam, Paul denies that he was deceived. Adam listened to Eve and sinned with his eyes wide open. Paul's point is that men, including those in Ephesus, are more susceptible to mistake and error when they carelessly surrender their God-given responsibilities to women.

A promise of obedient women (v. 15). But Paul expresses a promise for those women who showed obedience: "Women will be saved through childbearing." C. A. Trentham says Paul saw this truth most profoundly: "Woman's true fulfillment is in her devotion to that for which she was created, the bearing and rearing of children. . . . [This] is a loftier work for her even than being a leader in the church" (*Studies in Timothy*, Convention Press, 1959, p. 35).

■ *Both men and women must assume their*
■ *respective places of responsibility in the*
■ *church.*

1 TIMOTHY 3

CHURCH LEADERSHIP (3:1–13)

There seems to be no doubt that development took place in the organization of the church from the time of Paul's earlier epistles to the time when he wrote the Letters to Timothy and Titus. In 1 Cor. 12:4–10 and Rom. 12:6–8, the situation in the church seems to have been much more fluid and less organized than that reflected in the Pastoral Epistles.

In this section Paul discusses the qualifications of three groups of church leaders: (1) overseers or pastors, (2) deacons or church helpers, and (3) women helpers.

Qualifications of Overseers (vv. 1–7)

A commendation (v. 1). We have here the second of five "trustworthy sayings" in this letter: "If one is seeking the office of an overseer, he passionately desires a good work" (Wuest, p. 493).

Desiring this noble task or good work is only one of many qualifications.

Paul lists others.

An appeal for obedient behavior (vv. 2–3). The qualifications mentioned in verse 2 are largely positive and are traits that can be observed in one's behavior. The demands of verse 3 are negative. For a listing of these qualifications, see the chart below, "Qualifications of Overseers (Bishops)."

Leadership of the family (vv. 4–5). A church leader must "manage his own family well."

One of Paul's key points here is that the experience the leader gained in the home would develop sensitive compassion for this role in the church. The development of proper leadership skills in the home was a prerequisite for using them in the church.

An experienced leader (v. 6). Only the first converts to Christianity could assume office immediately after their conversion. Eventually, it would be important to select leaders with enough maturity to avoid the pitfalls of pride. The danger of appointing a recent convert to a place of leadership is that he may become a

"Manage"

The verb manage carries the idea of governing, leading, and giving direction to the family. It demands an effective exercise of authority bolstered by a character of integrity and compassion.

victim of the conceit that sometimes accompanies an important new position.

Respected by unbelievers (v. 7). An effective church leader needs the respect of even the unsaved world. If the behavior of the leader does not present a credible witness, the devil can entrap the church by making outsiders wary of believing the gospel. "Outsiders" are those who have not believed the gospel. A "good reputation" is literally a "good witness." Christians must realize that unbelievers scrutinize their actions with a searchlight. Paul's implied appeal is that church leaders give no opportunity for unbelievers genuinely to find fault.

Qualifications of Overseers (Bishops)

QUALIFICATION	EXPLANATION
Above reproach	a man of blameless character
Husband of one wife	faithful to his one wife
Temperate	free from rash actions
Self-controlled	a sensible person, trustworthy, and balanced in judgment
Respectable	demands dignity and orderliness in behavior
Hospitable	caring for Christians and others
Able to teach	competent and skillful in communicating Christian truth
Not given to drunkenness	controls his thirst for wine
Not violent but gentle	forbearing in relationships with troublemakers
Not quarrelsome	not contentious, grasping, pugnacious
Not a lover of money	not greedy
Manages his own family well	exemplary in controlling and directing his family unit; teaches his children obedience and respect

The Qualifications of Deacons (vv. 8–10, 12–13)

For a full list of qualifications, see p. 22.

Another appeal for obedience (vv. 8–9). Paul lists four requirements for the position of deacon.

On proven worth (v. 10). The demand for testing raises two questions. First, what is the nature of the testing? Paul does not clarify whether the examination of a candidate concerns doctrinal beliefs, moral practices, or a combination of both. The emphasis of verse 9 suggests that both doctrine and practice are important in Christianity.

Second, who does the testing? Again, Paul provides no specific statement. Acts 6:5 implies that the Seven were chosen by the congregation, but Titus 1:5 highlights the role of Titus in selecting leaders for the church at Crete. Perhaps a more mature congregation would act as a body in selecting its leaders, but a fledgling flock might rely on the wise insight of its founding pastor. The examination may have been informal, but the deacon-candidate needed to convince the church of his genuine Christian faith.

After the experience of testing, those who had "nothing against them" could serve as deacons.

Excelling at home (v. 12). Like overseers, deacons are to manage their children and their families well.

A promise for performance (v. 13). Deacons who serve well have the following two rewards:

1. He will receive an "excellent standing" for his effective service.
2. He will receive "great assurance." His confidence in Christ will grow.

Qualifications of Deacons (Church Helpers)

QUALIFICATION	EXPLANATION
Worthy of respect	serious–minded person whose character merits respect
Sincere	controlling speech; not engaging in double talk
Not indulging in much wine	does not love alcohol
Not pursuing dishonest gain	not given to questionable money-making
Hold to the truths of the faith with a clear conscience	has an inner guide to life that demonstrates obedience to God
Must first be tested	convinces church of his genuine Christian faith
Husband of one wife	faithful to his one wife
Manages children and household well	exemplary in controlling and directing his family unit; teaches his children obedience and respect

Qualifications of Women Helpers (v. 11)

The word *wives* is the same word translated "women" in 2:9–10 or "woman" in 2:11–12. The context will usually show whether the word refers to a married woman ("wife") or to the female gender ("women"). The question here is whether Paul was discussing the wives of the deacons, or was he presenting a special order of female helpers in Christian work?

New Testament Greek language did not have a special word for *deaconess*. Paul's failure to use a more specific title for these women was because there was not one in use at that time. His use of the term *wives* or *women* implies that these were women who helped the church in some manner. The early church did have women whose special responsibility was to work with women and children. They performed pastoral work with the sick and the poor and helped at baptism.

Paul outlines four requirements for a woman helper, which are detailed in the following chart.

Qualifications of Women Helpers

QUALIFICATION	EXPLANATION
Worthy of respect	exhibits character that merits respect
Not malicious talkers	The literal meaning of "malicious talker" is "slanderer" or "accuser"
Temperate	shows control or moderation in behavior
Trustworthy	is reliable and faithful

- Paul's appeals to the men and women leaders
- called for visible, mature, righteous living that
- commended Christianity to its observers. He
- wants them to show a maturity that has been
- proven by obedience and endurance under test-
- ing. God desires that the righteousness of spiri-
- tual leaders shine forth (Matt. 5:16) so the
- transforming power of Christianity might be
- evident for all to see (1 Tim. 3:7).

CORRECT APPLICATION OF CHRISTIAN TRUTH (3:14–16)

This passage serves as a bridge between the guidelines Paul gives in 2:1–3:13 and the warnings about false teaching that follow.

Paul's Plans for a Visit (v. 14)

Paul fully intends to make a visit "shortly" to Timothy in Ephesus. However, his travel plans were always subject to the will of God. Did Paul

"Shortly"

This adverb comes from the Greek word *tachos* which means "quickness" or "speed." We derive the word *tachometer*—a device that measures engine speed—from this *tachos*.

actually make his anticipated visit to Ephesus? Nothing in any of the Pastorals confirms that he made the journey.

Paul's Purpose for Writing (v. 15)

Paul's concern is for correct behavior in the church. He is interested in the relationships of people in God's "household," and he sets forth principles to guide those relationships. It is also apparent that "church" here has a broader connotation that just the local church at Ephesus. It includes the people of the living God, wherever they may be found.

The church has a responsibility for the truth. Paul speaks of the "pillar and foundation of the truth." That truth was under attack by people who were involved in wild speculations.

A Hymn for Believers (v. 16)

Christian truth is expressed in the central event of our faith—the event of the Incarnation. Several aspects of this truth are expressed in this hymn. (Paul probably did not compose this hymn but found it in the life of the church.) The hymn contains six distinct statements with Christ as the understood subject of each line.

Paul uses this hymn as an example of the mystery of godliness which the church proclaimed. This mystery relates to the Incarnation and Resurrection of Christ and the church's proclamation of the gospel.

What stands out is the simplicity of the mystery of godliness in comparison with complex speculations of false teachers.

Hymn for Believers

STATEMENT ABOUT CHRIST	SIGNIFICANCE
1. "He appeared in a body"	A reference to Jesus' Incarnation
2. "Was vindicated by the Spirit"	Recalls the statements about Christ's Resurrection
3. "Was seen by angels"	A reference to the worship given by angels to the ascended Christ
4. "Was preached among the nations"	Refers to the proclamation of the gospel among the nations of the world
5. "Was believed on in the world"	Described as the response to the proclamation
6. "Was taken up in glory"	A reference to the brightness and majesty of God's presence in Jesus

Christians are to distinguish themselves by a lifestyle of holiness. Believers are those whose behavior designates them as God's children and demonstrates the reality of their faith. They are to build their lives on the strong foundation of the gospel.

GUIDING QUESTIONS

1. Compare the positions of overseer and deacons in the church. What is the function of each? What are the responsibilities of each?

2. What were the roles of women helpers in the early church?

3. What is the promise of reward to deacons for effective service?

4. What is the focus of Paul's "Hymn for Believers"? What might we learn from reflecting on it?

One perennial idea that came from certain schools of Greek philosophy was that the spirit was good while matter was evil. When these concepts intersected with Christian teaching, numerous distortions of the faith occurred.

Apostasy

Apostasy is the act of rebelling against, forsaking, abandoning, or falling away from what one has believed. Our English word *apostasy* is derived from a Greek word that means "to stand away from." Paul taught that apostasy would precede the Day of the Lord. The Holy Spirit has explicitly revealed this falling away from the faith (1 Tim. 4:1). Such apostasy in the latter times will involve doctrinal deception, moral insensitivity, and ethical departures from God's truth.

UNDERSTANDING FALSE PRACTICE (4:1–5)

The Christian faith was preached, accepted, and lived out in a world where many ideas threatened it. There is always a danger of the gospel being distorted either by adding to it or taking something from it. In this passage, Paul elaborates on the errors in Ephesus and calls on Timothy to oppose them.

A Warning against Apostasy (vv. 1–3)

The Holy Spirit has expressly warned that some people will fall away from the faith. Rather than focusing on the profound simplicity of the gospel, they will turn aside and give attention to spirits who will deceive them and to doctrines promoted by demons. The spokespersons for these deceptions are people who are given to hypocrisy and lying. The result of this behavior is that their consciences no longer work as God intended, but they have literally been cauterized as if by a branding iron.

Paul calls his readers' attention to two features that characterize the teaching of the false teachers: (1) forbidding marriage, and (2) abstaining from certain foods.

An Argument against Asceticism (v. 4)

Paul rejects any division of foods into two categories— good and evil. He presents two reasons why this division should not occur. First, he affirms that God's Creation is good. All that God has made is good. The facts of God's benevolent Creation implies that we can eat all that God has made. Second, we must eat with thanksgiving what God has created.

An Argument for Blessing Food (v. 5)

Paul was probably suggesting that in responding to the gospel, the believers in Ephesus had learned that there are no food laws. The gospel had brought them into a proper understanding of food, and they acknowledged by prayer that it was a gift from God. This act of blessing the food made it special or consecrated before God.

■ *Paul describes a destructive legalism in this*
■ *section. This legalism prevented one's grasp of*
■ *the freedom and power of the Holy Spirit, and*
■ *it destroyed gratitude toward God. Legalism,*
■ *however, cannot endure long in the presence of*
■ *an attitude of gratitude to God.*

TIMOTHY'S PERFORMANCE OF HIS TASK (4:6–16)

Facing Falsehood (vv. 6–10)

What should be our strategy when we live in a world inundated with false teaching? Paul teaches that we must (1) expose the errors we oppose; and (2) develop personal holiness to assure continuation in integrity. The combination of exposing error and practicing truth is a powerful antidote to heresy.

Demonstrating Christian Behavior (vv. 11–16)

Timothy had begun well in obeying God's commands. Paul desired that he continue in the path he had started in order to provide an example for others.

Timothy was possibly a timid young man. His timidity could hinder him from making a bold assertion of Christian truth. Paul wanted Timothy to speak with authority. He wanted Timothy to "teach these things." By issuing the directives and instruction of 4:6–10, Paul provided several emphases that should characterize Timothy's ministry:

- Timothy was to live as a spiritual example of what a believer truly can be.
- He was to apply himself to reading, preaching, and teaching.
- He was not to neglect the spiritual gift he had received.
- He was to be consistent in his spiritual growth.

S̹N

The best antidote for error is a positive presentation of the truth. As a teacher of the truth, Timothy was to demonstrate a personal godliness that he might be a living example to his congregation. Church members will follow someone whom they respect.

GUIDING QUESTIONS

1. What did the false teachers teach? What was Paul's response?
2. What are practical ways for the church to guard the gospel from heresy and false teachers?
3. What is *apostasy*? How is it evident in our churches today? What should be our course of action to address it?
4. What actions did Paul emphasize when instructing Timothy on how to perform his tasks?

RESPONSIBILITIES TOWARD CHURCH GROUPS (5:1–16)

The New Testament has many metaphors for the church. One of the most meaningful is the family of God. How is the younger minister to relate to the various age groups in his church? Paul takes his cue from relationships in the family. He requests treatment that recognizes these family relationships.

Paul gives Timothy directions for meeting the needs of three groups within the church at Ephesus.

Proper Treatment for All Ages (vv. 1–2)

Older men. Paul urges Timothy not to rebuke an older man.

The youthful Timothy faced a delicate situation in appealing to older men, but the difference between their ages did not make admonition of these men any less necessary.

"Rebuke"

The term *rebuke* used here occurs nowhere else in the New Testament; it describes a severe verbal pounding. Such treatment would show no appreciation for age.

Younger men. Timothy was not to "talk down" to younger men, but he was to treat them as equals. The term *exhort* demands a kindlier, more considerate approach than "rebuke." Those who err would need to receive some rebuke for their behavior, but Timothy is to avoid a pompous approach in relating to them.

Older women. Paul directs Timothy to treat the older women respectfully as mothers (Rom. 16:13). A church leader would find it virtually impossible to heap verbal abuse on an older woman if he shows respect for her.

Younger women. Younger women posed a special problem for Timothy. He was to treat them as sisters and maintain a purity that would banish

"Religion that God accepts is this: caring for orphans or widows who need help; and keeping yourself free from the world's evil influence" (James 1:27, NCV).

all evil in thought and deed. "Purity" calls for modesty and chastity in all relationships.

The Care of True Widows (vv. 3–8)

Paul identifies two types of widows: those who had relatives to care for them and those who had no living family members. Those who had family were to receive support from their family. Caring for one's own family should have high priority in a Christian's life.

Those who fail to do so deny the faith and are worse than unbelievers (v. 8) who may have a better track record of caring for their families.

The true widow. Paul describes the true widow—one who is really in need—with three phrases. His description outlines more precisely the kind of person whom Paul had exhorted Timothy to honor. The true widow is one who:

1. *Was "left all alone."* She had no relatives to support her and no source of income or encouragement.
2. *"Puts her hope in God."* She has developed a settled and continuous confidence in God. The Williams translation words it: "has fixed her hope on God."
3. *Was a woman of prayer who prayed "night and day."* This phrase is a metaphor describing a person who prays continually.

The opposite of this ministry of prayer is the life of self-indulgence or pleasure. The widow who abandons herself to pleasure and comfort is in complete contrast with the godly widow who prays and seeks God. A widow, supported by the church, could not use her idle time in seeking self-gratification. Paul was aware of this possibility and felt that steps should be taken to guard against it.

ℕ

■ *Three terms sum up this section: respect,*
■ *compassion, and responsibility. Paul speaks*
■ *to the church and individual families about*
■ *the urgency for showing compassion to truly*
■ *needy widows. At the center of what it means*
■ *to be a Christian is the responsibility of pro-*
■ *viding material support for the helpless*
■ *members of one's own family.*

A Warning to Younger Widows (vv. 9–16)

Paul's chief concern in this section is to single out the younger widows who were apparently a source of great difficulty for the Ephesian church (2 Tim. 5:15). Paul recommends the behavior of true widows as a desirable contrast to the actions of the frivolous younger widows.

Paul names three basic requirements for anyone on this list:

1. The widow could not be less than sixty years of age.
2. The widow must have been "faithful to her husband."
3. Specific works should characterize the life of the widow.

These "works" are actions the widow must already have performed and on which her reputation was based. The younger widows failed to meet these requirements.

Therefore, Paul states that the younger widows should not be counted among the true widows. The younger widows, therefore, are encouraged to remarry and fulfill the functions of wife and mother.

The point of verse 16 is that relatives should assume responsibility for the widows in their families. This would free the churches to use their meager resources for the widows who were left completely alone in the world.

- ■ *The younger widows do not meet the require-*
- ■ *ments of a true widow. Therefore, Paul encour-*
- ■ *ages the younger widows to remarry and urges*
- ■ *them to assume the responsible behavior*
- ■ *appropriate to a married woman rather than*
- ■ *the idle, meddling actions of a tattletale.*

THE PROPER HANDLING OF LEADERS (5:17–25)

Recognition and Discipline of Leaders (vv. 17–20)

Recognition (vv. 17–18). An elder who showed himself proficient in leadership was "worthy of double honor." *Honor* means pay or financial remuneration. Simply stated, it means the best leader should get twice as much. Paul asks that special consideration be given to those who labored in "preaching and teaching." The ministry of the Word was the highest responsibility of all.

Paul quotes two biblical sources in support of this command: "You shall not muzzle the ox while he is threshing" (Deut. 25:4 NASB), and "the laborer is worthy of his wages" (Mark 10:7, NASB).

Discipline (vv. 19–20). Paul discusses the process of discipline for erring leaders. First, he warns against accepting an accusation against an elder unless two or three witnesses support it. Paul is not urging special treatment for the elder, but he is urging fair protection from any capricious accusations.

Those who continued to sin after being warned in private should be rebuked before the entire congregation. The open rebuke was designed to change the course of the erring pastor's life as well as to put the fear of God within the entire congregation.

■ *Today's churches resemble the church in*
■ *Ephesus in that they have leaders who*
■ *deserve recognition as well as those who*
■ *merit correction. Paul provides advice for*
■ *recognizing those leaders who do their job*
■ *well and instructions for dealing with those*
■ *elders who face accusation. Paul's goal is to*
■ *avoid partiality toward important leaders*
■ *and to provide fair treatment for all.*

Paul is here drawing on a time-honored principle of justice among God's people: "On the evidence of two witnesses or three witnesses, he who is to die shall be put to death; he shall not be put to death on the evidence of one witness" (Deut. 17:6, NASB)

Special Directions to Timothy (vv. 21–25)

Paul now charges Timothy to assume initiative in handling the problems of church leadership. This charge involves several elements.

1. *He warns Timothy of making hasty appointments to Christian offices.* He hints that one who participates in such an appointment shares in the sinful results that can easily follow.

2. *He appeals for personal purity in Timothy.* "Purity" involves separation from immorality and single-mindedness of purpose.

3. *He urges Timothy to "use a little wine" for his apparent stomach ailment.* Contaminated water may have aggravated Timothy's problems. Wine was widely used for such medicinal purposes.

4. *He warns Timothy against hasty acceptance and hasty rejection of the "sins" of the elders.* Paul did not believe that evil could remain hidden forever in God's order.

Nor did he believe that goodness would be covered up ultimately.

■ *The church has a responsibility for the moral*
■ *quality of its leadership. That responsibility*
■ *is limited, however, because our knowledge*
■ *of the good and evil in others is limited.*
■ *Eventually, all will be apparent. We may be*
■ *sure of this, for God, the ultimate Judge,*
■ *knows our hearts.*

GUIDING QUESTIONS

1. What relationship did Paul see between the older and younger men?
2. What did relationship did Paul see between the older and younger women?
3. What is the church's responsibility for the care of widows?
4. What practical advice does Paul give Timothy for handling the problems of their church leadership?

1 TIMOTHY 6

A WARNING TO SLAVES AND SINNERS (6:1–10)

The Responsibility of Christian Slaves (vv. 1–2a)

The phrase "under the yoke" describes the galling, humiliating result of slavery. Paul insists, however, that Christian slaves are to have a genuine respect for their owners. This would produce an outward expression in word, manner, and performance. The great object of Paul's con-

"Many members of the early church were slaves. The question arises, Why does Paul seem to countenance slavery? It must be remembered that a direct attack upon the practice would have caused misunderstanding in the church and would probably have led to an ineffectual, open rebellion against a deeply entrenched institution, which would, no doubt, have resulted in widespread suffering" (C. A. Trentham in *Studies in Timothy*, Convention Press, 1959, p. 68).

cern was the glory of God. Bad behavior by professing Christian slaves could only lead an owner to mock Christianity.

Slaves who have Christian masters are to honor them and not be disrespectful to them or presumptuous with them because they are brothers in Christ. Rather, they should show all the more respect to them.

- *Regarding slaves, Paul did not emphasize indi-*
- *vidual rights but individual responsibilities.*
- *His chief concern was the glory of God, not the*
- *liberation of the slaves or an increase in the*
- *privilege for the owners. Equality before God*
- *does not guarantee that all human beings enjoy*
- *equal roles or life status. While Paul accepted a*
- *different status for master and slave, he*
- *demanded a changed attitude from both.*

An Indictment of the False Teachers (vv. 2b–5)

After a brief diversion to deal with the servant-master relationship, Paul exposes further the shortcomings of the false teachers. "These . . . things," which Paul urges Timothy to teach most likely refer to the teachings Paul has enunciated throughout this letter. The unhealthy teaching of the false teachers stand in contrast to the healthy instruction from Jesus' teaching. (This is a rare reference in the Epistles to the actual teachings of Jesus.)

Paul mentions three unhealthy traits of the false teachers:

1. They were pompous or "conceited."
2. Despite their arrogance, they lacked genuine spiritual knowledge.

3. They were ailing with the disease of controversy and word battles.

Paul goes on to describe the products of their impaired instruction. These include an envy that shows annoyance at the success of others and feeds a spirit of dissension. Also included are "malicious talk," wicked denunciations of others, "evil suspicions," faultfinding, and misgivings about the integrity of others. The vividness of Paul's description suggests that he was facing a concrete situation that aroused his indignant protest. Paul saw that a sense of real community had been destroyed.

Paul's last criticism is a devastating one. He accuses the false teachers of being motivated by a desire for "financial gain." From early on, the Christian religion was seized upon by people for personal exploitation. These were men of "corrupt mind, who have been robbed of the truth."

The Greed of the False Teachers (vv. 6–10)

Paul's accusation about the profiteering motive of the false teachers leads to his statements about the relation between the believer and money. Genuine Christian faith brings great gain when coupled with contentment.

In these verses Paul shows two reasons for which contentment should be a companion to godliness, and then explains the desire for wealth as a trap that plunges the unwary into spiritual ruin.

Why do godliness and contentment represent great gain? Paul offers two reasons:

1. *After a brief stay, we shall depart this life as we came in.* It is sheer folly to concern ourselves with earthly matters. Material gain is irrelevant, and greed is irrational.

Contentment

The word contentment means "to be sufficient in oneself, adequate, and needing no assistance." It expresses the essence of the Stoic ideal, which was to be independent of external circumstances. Paul Christianized this term, using it to refer to an attitude of mind independent of externals and dependent only on God. He was not advocating godless self-sufficiency as a source of contentment. Rather, Paul believed that true sufficiency is Christ-sufficiency (Phil. 4:13).

2. *We must be content when we possess life's necessities.* Paul is contrasting the believer's attitude with that of the greedy heretics. His words reflect the teaching of Jesus (Matt. 6:25–34).

Paul also warns that the greedy person becomes entrapped by the snare of his own desires. The end of such people is "ruin and destruction." Paul paints three progressive pitfalls in which the willful wealth-seeker becomes entangled:

1. Wealth tempts like a lure and causes people to covet the wrong objects.

2. Individuals become entangled like animals dangling in a trap.

3. The trapped ones drown in an almost personified wealth that becomes a "personal monster."

- Godliness is not a trait from which to make
- material profit. True godliness has content-
- ment for its companion. Since we cannot take
- life's luxuries into God's presence, we should
- be content with basic necessities

INSTRUCTIONS TO TIMOTHY AND THE WEALTHY (6:11–21)

A Program for Godliness (vv. 11–16)

Paul's statements in this section consist of a series of commands, a solemn charge, and an outpouring of praise to God.

Commands for Timothy. Paul delivers several commands to Timothy to warn and challenge him regarding the task ahead:

"For the love of money"

Paul supports his warning about wealth with a contemporary proverb: "For the love of money is a root of all kinds of evil" (v. 10). The Greek text does not say "the love of money is the root of all evils." Literally, it says that it is a root of evil. It is one of the sources of evil. We can make three general observations about this proverb:

1. It does not condemn money but rather the love of money.

2. It does not state that all evil comes from the love of money, but such misplaced love can cause a great variety of evil.

3. The wandering elders from Ephesus who had sold out to greed were living proof of this maxim.

1. *Flee* the heresy of the false teachers. Timothy was to stand in contrast to the false teachers.

2. *Pursue* the six virtues that Paul lists. The Williams New Testament translates "pursue" as "constantly strive for," expressing the grammatical force of the verb. The list of virtues includes righteousness, godliness, faith, love, endurance, and gentleness.

3. *Fight* the good fight of faith. To fight for "the faith" includes a least a struggle for the truth of the gospel, but it may also refer to the whole of Timothy's Christian life as a great contest requiring discipline and purpose.

4. *Take hold* of eternal life. Timothy was to continue in the contest until it ended in triumphant conclusion. Depending on the context, eternal life could be a blessing to be realized at the journey's end or a present experience.

Charge. Paul's charge in the presence of God and of Jesus Christ to Timothy was to keep the "command" until Jesus returns. It may refer to directives given to Timothy at his baptism or during the laying on of hands. Or, it may be a commandment to Timothy to persevere in his own faith and ministry. He reminded Timothy that Jesus' good confession before Pontius Pilate was his model.

An Outpouring of Praise to God. Paul expresses seven statements of majestic praise to God in a moving doxology. In verse 15, he uses three titles in a description of God. In verse 16 he focuses on God's divine essence. All these phrases are Jewish in style, uniquely expressing the sovereignty of God.

"And Pilate questioned him, "Are You the King of the Jews?" And answering He said to him, 'It is as you say.' And the chief priests began to accuse Him harshly. And Pilate was questioning Him again, saying, "Do You make no answer? See how many charges they bring against You!' But Jesus made no further answer; so that Plate was amazed"(Mark 15:2–5 NASB).

Paul's Doxology

STATEMENT OF PRAISE		MEANING
"Blessed and only ruler"	Title	God has the universal authority to decide the precise time of Christ's return
"King of kings"	Title	God's sovereign authority over all powers, both human and divine
"Lord of lords"	Title	Same as for "King of kings"
"Immortal"	Attribute	God is self-existent and so One who will not die
Glory ("unapproachable light")	Attribute	God is unapproachable physically by human beings
"Honor"	Attribute	God's worthiness in receiving esteem and reverence
"Might"	Attribute	The power of God expressed in sovereign acts

■ *Paul provides positive action for Timothy to*
■ *undertake after warning him to flee the evil*
■ *desire for wealth. Paul's practice was wise*
■ *and sensible. He prohibits Timothy's pursuit*
■ *of wealth, but urges him to follow hard after*
■ *the traits of righteousness and godliness and*
■ *to continue the struggle for the truth of the*
■ *gospel in the Christian life.*

A Promise for the Prosperous (vv. 17–19)

From the available evidence, we conclude that the churches did not have many rich members. As time went on, however, their number probably grew as the churches grew. This passage shows that some believers, at least, had to deal with the temptation presented by wealth.

One problem of riches was its threat to Christian fellowship. So Paul contrasts the right and

Stop storing up your riches on earth where moths and rust make away with them, and where thieves break in and steal them. But keep on storing up your riches in heaven where moths and rust do not make away with them and where thieves do not break in and steal them. For wherever your treasure is, there too your heart will be. (Matt. 6:19–21, Williams)

wrong responses to wealth. A rich person might be tempted to be "arrogant" toward the poor or to make wealth the hope of one's life.

In contrast, Paul mentions four ways to use wealth wisely:

1. *"To do good."* This involves using wealth in a positive way instead of letting it feed a life of personal luxury.
2. *"To be rich in good deeds."* This points the wealthy in the direction in which they are to be truly rich.
3. *"To be generous."* This demands a liberal sharing of wealth with others.
4. *"To be willing to share."* This shows that the generous act of giving is to spring up from internal generosity.

The outcome of this kind of generosity is two-fold: (1) the giver stores up treasure for the coming age; and (2) it allows the giver to lay hold of eternal life here and now.

■ *Paul urges the wealthy to enrich their lives with*
■ *all kinds of good deeds. He particularly urges*
■ *them to share their wealth to help the needy.*

A Concluding Caution (vv. 20–21)
This final exhortation to Timothy once again involves both the positive and negative aspects of Christian living.

"Guard"

Paul exhorts Timothy to guard what has been entrusted to him. Literally, this is "guard the deposit." The "deposit" is a banking term denoting a sum deposited to the responsibility of a bank. (Compare the same word used in 2 Tim. 1:12, 14.)

1. Timothy is to "guard" the genuine teachings of the gospel. They have been given to him as a trust. In each generation, much depends on the faithfulness of the ministers to that trust.
2. Timothy is to "turn away from godless chatter." He is to avoid the kinds of ideas

that have threatened the sound teachings of the faith. The "knowledge" of the heretics included empty fables, genealogies, and asceticism.

In this tension in which Timothy found himself, he needed "grace" above all. He needed the presence, help, and love of a gracious God. That's exactly what Paul wished for him in the closing words of the letter.

GUIDING QUESTIONS

1. The role of a slave during the days of the early church was often difficult. What warnings and exhortations did Paul give to Christian slaves?

2. Describe the unhealthy traits of the false teachers. What was the result of their teaching to others? How did it affect some of the Ephesian believers? What is the Christian view of contentment?

3. Describe God's "program for godliness" for Timothy. Might today's young pastors heed these same commands and Pauline exhortations?

2 TIMOTHY 1

SALUTATION (1:1–2)

Paul wrote his second letter to Timothy from the loneliness of a dungeon while awaiting death (4:6–8). Paul's salutation is brief and similar to that of 1 Timothy. The apostle gave a lengthy salutation to Titus; but in this, his final letter, he uses a standard form.

The Author (v. 1)

Paul speaks of himself as an "apostle." This is a term that refers to one selected by God to serve as an ambassador to herald the approach of the gospel. He uses the term to lend credibility to his directives for Timothy, which reinforces Paul's urgent appeals to Timothy to heed and follow Paul and his gospel.

Timothy's Spiritual Lineage

Timothy's grandmother Lois and mother Eunice had been women of sincere faith. To know and be influenced by persons of this caliber is one of God's greatest gifts. Paul met these women and got to know them well on his first and second missionary journeys to Lystra.

The Recipient (v. 2a)

In 1 Timothy, Paul addresses Timothy as "my dear son." That expression underscores the special relationship between the older apostle and the younger helper. It also gives a public legitimacy to Timothy before the Ephesian church.

The Greeting (v. 2b)

Paul uses the identical wording for expressing the greeting here and in 1 Timothy: "grace, mercy, and peace." Each of these words has special meaning for Paul's readers:

Grace. This describes the gracious goodness that God offers to undeserving sinners.

Mercy. This is God's help offered to the discouraged and stumbling (Heb. 4:16).

Peace. This describes a state of salvation that results from the grace and mercy of God.

PAUL'S GRATITUDE (1:3–5)

Paul's letters ordinarily include a thanksgiving at the beginning. His gratitude to God for Timothy is a consistent element in prayers for his younger associate. Paul served the God whom his "forefathers" served. Both he and his ancestors were loyal to the same God and were involved in the same redemptive purpose.

The last parting between Paul and Timothy had been painful and emotional. Paul vividly remembers Timothy's tears. He experienced constant longing to be reunited with his friend and fellow servant of Christ.

One of the character traits which attracted Paul to Timothy and which gave Paul confidence in entrusting the work of the gospel to him was Timothy's sincere faith. Although our faith doesn't come from our family, a godly family provides the environment in which a sincere faith can flourish.

QUALITIES NEEDED IN MINISTRY (1:6–18)

A Call for Courage (vv. 6–7)

Paul's conviction that Timothy had genuine faith leads him to urge Timothy to fan his gift into an open flame. The gift to which Paul refers is Timothy's gift for ministry. Timothy had to function in an environment of fear, heresy, and challenges to his leadership. His gift related to administration and organization rather than evangelization.

Throughout this epistle, Paul pictures Timothy as a younger and more hesitant colleague. He

The tears Paul remembers Timothy shedding may have been on the occasion when Paul met the Ephesian Christians at Miletus just before Paul traveled to Jerusalem for the last time.

Luke describes the parting as follows: "And when he [Paul] had said these things, he knelt down and prayed with them all. And they began to weep aloud and embraced Paul, and repeatedly kissed him, grieving especially over the word which he had spoken, that they should see his face no more. And they were accompanying him to the ship" (Acts 20: 36–38 NASB).

"The laying on of . . . hands"

This is a reference to a time when Timothy's gifts were officially recognized. Paul focused only on his role in the recognition of Timothy's gifts because he wanted to emphasize the close personal relationship between himself and Timothy. The act of laying on of hands was symbolic. It was not the cause of Timothy's receipt of a spiritual gift, but it was a visible representation and symbol of it.

reminds Timothy of his spiritual gift for ministry in order to encourage a revitalized commitment. This is not so much a command as a reminder. Paul's approach to Timothy shows the gentleness of a seasoned pastor.

Paul's reference to the "spirit" does not refer to the Holy Spirit, but to those traits of which the Spirit is the author. These traits represent gifts for performing special ministries. The Holy Spirit does not produce "timidity" or cowardice. A spirit of cowardice would falter under the load of responsibility Paul was placing on Timothy. Instead, the Holy Spirit produces three special gifts:

1. *Power*—a reference to a forcefulness of character that can use authority boldly and fulfill difficult tasks.
2. *Love*—a love that endures even the most cantankerous opposition, conquering opposition by forgiveness and a refusal to seek revenge.
3. *Self-discipline*—to correct and warn the wayward and careless.

- *Paul calls on Timothy to demonstrate courage. His conviction that Timothy had genuine faith leads him to urge Timothy to fan his gift of ministry into an open flame. The Holy Spirit would provide three gifts for performing special ministries—power, love, and self-discipline—that would enable Timothy to carry out his mission.*

A Readiness to Suffer (vv. 8–12)

Now we come to the point of Paul's concern. He was aware that Timothy was being tested by those opposing the genuine gospel of Jesus Christ.

Paul appeals to Timothy to join Paul in suffering for the gospel. First, the epistle mentions two truths of the gospel that would promote a readiness to endure hardship for Jesus. Second, he refers to features of his own life that would provide an example for Timothy to imitate:

1. *The gospel provides access to divine power.* Paul outlines the process of salvation, the purpose of salvation, and the basis of salvation:

   Process—a call from God to share in His kingdom, outwardly by the preaching of the gospel; inwardly by the Spirit working through the Word.

   Purpose—that each believer might produce a life of obedience and holiness to God instead of self.

   Basis—is the purpose and grace of God, not human merit.

2. *The powerful effect of the gospel.* Paul now moves to a discussion of God's purposes in eternity to Christ's appearance in time. He makes three points:

   God's plan to save has been revealed by Jesus' appearance as Savior. God's saving power through Christ has been at work before the world was founded. Christ is the Mediator through whom the divine grace comes to human beings.

   Jesus has destroyed death. He put death out of action. Although Christians are not released from physical death, their approach to it means that it is no longer

"I know"

"The word 'know' is not *ginosko*, 'experiential knowledge,' but *oida*, 'absolute, beyond a peradventure of a doubt knowledge, ' the latter being the stronger word. The knowledge here is not personal knowledge gained by experience, such as fellowship with God, but a knowledge of what God is in Himself which makes Him absolutely dependable in any circumstances." (Kenneth S. Wuest, *The Pastoral Epistles in the Greek New Testament,* Eerdmans, p. 123).

to be feared (Heb. 2:14–15), and it has lost its sting (1 Cor. 15:55).

Jesus has "brought life and immortality to light through the gospel." The resurrection of Christ brought eternal life and immortality out into the open for the first time where people could see it. What had been a hope was now a certainty.

It was for proclamation of this good news that Paul suffered, but he was not ashamed to do so. He knew the one whom he believed. Knowing Christ, Paul knew that the deposit he had made with Him was secure—Christ would keep it until that day—the *day* of his appearing once again.

An Imitation of Paul's Example (vv. 13–14)

Knowing Christ's absolute dependability, Paul calls on Timothy to mirror that dependability by adhering to the pattern of sound words which Paul imparted to Timothy and by guarding that deposit with the help of the Holy Spirit.

The task of preserving the truth of the gospel is so demanding and difficult that human strength alone cannot assure it. Maintaining the purity of the gospel demands the might and wisdom of the Holy Spirit.

These sound and saving words are to be communicated to the churches not just as words but in the faith and love of Christ.

An Incentive for Faithfulness (vv. 15–18)

An example of disloyalty. A poignant, personal note intrudes at this point. The apostle in prison was saddened because he had been deserted by people who should have supported him. We do not know at what point the people in the province of Asia turned against him.

Paul grieves at this neglect, but the encouragement Onesiphorus gave him greatly cheers him. Paul wants Timothy to imitate the example of Onesophorus and avoid the shame of those who had deserted him.

What was the nature of the desertion? These former friends of Paul had turned against him personally, but they also seem to have rejected the gospel he preached. We know nothing more about either Phygelus or Hermogenes from Scripture.

An example of loyalty. In contrast to the behavior of the profane pair above was the commendable behavior of Onesiphorus. Paul speaks affectionately of his diligent, unselfish service. What is unclear is the situation Onesiphorus faced. Was he alive or deceased?

Paul prayed that Onesiphorus would "find mercy from the Lord on that day!" (the day of judgment). This underlies the fact that he, like all others, must depend solely on the mercy of God in the future judgment.

■ *Paul also calls on Timothy to demonstrate a*
■ *readiness to suffer for the cause of Christ. Paul*
■ *was not ashamed to present himself as the ini-*
■ *tial example for Timothy. Ultimately, moral*
■ *behavior cannot be taught by character-build-*
■ *ing courses. Christians must see moral commit-*
■ *ment as a sterling example in others.*

GUIDING QUESTIONS

1. What are Paul's circumstances as he writes this letter? What is the basis of his gratitude?

In other literature (the apocryphal book, Acts of Paul and Thecla), Phygelus and Hermogenes are described as "full of hypocrisy." They may have served as ringleaders of the trouble in Ephesus along with Hymenaeus and Philetus (2 Tim. 2:17–18).

Onesiphorus

His name means "profit bearing." Ephesian Christians praised his effort to seek out the place of Paul's arrest, his disregard of the shame connected with befriending one in chains, and his past service in Ephesus (2 Tim. 1:16–18). The greeting of and prayer for the household of Onesiphorus has suggested to some that Onesiphorus was already dead. All that can be assumed is that Onesiphorus was not at Ephesus.

2. What gifts from the Holy Spirit did Timothy rely on for performing special ministry? Might today's minister expect the same kind of strength and resources from the Spirit?

3. What does a "laying on of hands" signify?

4. What truths about the gospel promote a readiness to suffer?

2 TIMOTHY 2

IMAGES OF EFFECTIVENESS IN MINISTRY (2:1–7)

After appealing for qualities such as courage, willingness to suffer, and faithfulness in the life of a minister, Paul borrows images from daily life to illustrate the traits necessary for effective service. He pictures a teacher, a soldier, an athlete, and a farmer.

The Teacher (vv. 1–2)

Paul charges Timothy to send on faithfully the message he had received. Paul demanded Timothy's active involvement in the training of a future generation of Christian servants.

To be equal to this task, Paul challenges Timothy to be strong in the grace of Christ Jesus.

The "things."

These are the foundational truths of the gospel Timothy is to send to trustworthy believers. These men needed to be able to pass along these truths to others by their ability and willingness to teach.

"Be strong"

This is a vigorous word that implies which Timothy is to keep on being empowered by God. Paul's command demands Timothy's continuous active cooperation with God. "Keep in touch with the power" (A. T. Robertson, *WPNT,* IV, p. 616).

The Soldier (vv. 3–4)

Because of the soldierlike hardship of life, Timothy desperately needed an abundant supply of grace which Paul describes.

Paul uses the imagery of the soldier to make at least three points:

1. *Spiritual growth.* To commend growth or accomplishment in some aspect of Christian behavior (1 Cor. 9:7; Phil 2:25).

2. *Proper ambition.* To show that the soldier's ambition must be that of pleasing the commander.

3. *Right priorities.* To show the importance of developing an ability to distinguish between doing *good* things and doing the *best* things.

The Athlete (v. 5)

Paul uses the picture of an athlete to illustrate the importance of complete devotion and stamina in Christian living. Performing as an athlete demands a commitment to a regimen of training and to the rules for the game.

Paul implies to Timothy that the Christian athlete could expect suffering, but he also holds out the promise of a prize for the committed athlete. In the Pastoral Epistles, Paul uses athletic images in 1 Tim. 4:7–8; 6:12 in order to emphasize that the Christian life demands the practice of self-discipline, affecting both personal behavior and inner attitude.

Christians must practice self-control. Each Christian must also have an inner preparedness to endure cheerfully the demands and hardships that spiritual commitment will bring (cf. 1 Cor. 9:24–27).

"In the grace."

Paul shows the need for living by the means of God's grace and constantly within the sphere of strength given by God's grace. "Christ is the dynamo for power only when and while we keep in touch with Him" (A. T. Robertson, *WPNT*, IV p. 616).

"Endure hardship with us"

This phrase is a two-word compound ("with" + "suffer hardship") that means literally "to suffer together with someone" or "to take one's share of suffering hardship." The text mentions no specific person with whom Timothy was to share this suffering, Goodspeed's translation, "join the ranks of those who bear suffering" catches the sense of the command.

The Farmer (v. 6)

Paul uses the analogy of a farmer to show that the one who works hard has first claim on the fruits of the work. Paul frequently uses the verb "hardworking" to describe the work of ministry. The farmer who works hard will be the first to enjoy the fruits, and the diligent Christian servant can expect the same.

This passage emphasizes the anticipation of a final reward from the Lord for earnest, steady work in Christ's service. The time of enjoyment of these fruits is in the future, at the time of Christ's return (2 Cor. 5:10).

The Application (v. 7)

 Paul asks Timothy to reflect on these images, and emphasizes the traits that believers need to demonstrate their service for the Lord. These include:

- Faithful skills of a competent teacher
- The willingness to suffer and the priority choices of a soldier
- The self-discipline of an athlete, and
- The hard work of a farmer.

As we also reflect on these images, God will provide the understanding for applying these truths.

Effective ministry requires such qualities as courage, willingness to suffer, and faithfulness in the life of a minister. The positive images Paul presents—teacher, soldier, athlete, and farmer—demand our consideration and reflection for their proper application in our lives.

TRUTHS THAT PROMOTE
EFFECTIVENESS IN MINISTRY (2:8–13)

A Proper Understanding of Christ (v. 8)

Paul now urges Timothy to rivet his attention on Christ, mentioning two features of Christ's person and work:

1. *He emphasizes Christ's resurrection.* Jesus' resurrection from the dead is the prime example of victory over death. It provides an encouragement for any believer who faces suffering.
2. *He points out that Christ "descended from David."* This shows that Christ has messianic qualifications and is the Heir to the glorious promises of God for David.

The memory of Christ cloaked with resurrection power and messianic dignity is an inspiration for Christian service.

The Goal of Paul's Suffering (vv. 9–10)

Paul explains the aim of his suffering. He had suffered so as to enable God's chosen people (the "elect") to obtain their salvation. "God's word is not chained" is Paul's way of saying that while people could silence him, they could not silence the power of God's Word (Phil. 1:12–18). This is a reminder that, above all, the spread of the gospel is a work of divine power (2 Tim. 1:7).

The knowledge that the gospel was not chained or bound provides Paul with an incentive to endure.

The Certainty of Reward (vv. 11–13)

These verses are another of Paul's "trustworthy sayings" (cf. 1 Tim. 1:15; 3:1; 4:9). (For additional treatment of these, see commentary on 1 Tim. 1:15 in this volume.)

This saying is structured by four conditional statements, each starting with the word "if." Each statement describes an action of a believer.

A Trustworthy Saying

CONDITION	CONCLUSION
"If we died with Him"	"we will also live with Him."
"If we endure"	"we will also reign with Him."
"If we disown Him"	"He will also disown us."
"If we are faithless"	"He will remain faithful."

Paul's main point with this section is the faithfulness of God. Paul wants to make it very clear that this is an area where no parallel exists. Human beings are often unfaithful. God is never unfaithful. Human faithlessness only serves to decorate God's faithfulness. We can always trust Him to act according to His character and promises.

Paul's certainty of reward derives largely from the certainty that God was faithful to care for and love His people. God's faithfulness means future life and glory for believers.

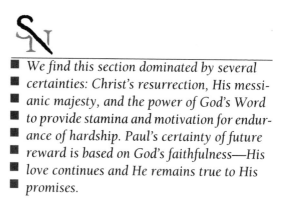

■ *We find this section dominated by several*
■ *certainties: Christ's resurrection, His messi-*
■ *anic majesty, and the power of God's Word*
■ *to provide stamina and motivation for endur-*
■ *ance of hardship. Paul's certainty of future*
■ *reward is based on God's faithfulness—His*
■ *love continues and He remains true to His*
■ *promises.*

THE CONFUSION OF FALSE TEACHING AND LIVING (2:14–26)

Resistance of the False Teachers (vv. 14–19)

Paul's opening appeal is for Timothy to do his duty for the people. He is to remind his audience continually to endure in their commitment while proclaiming the Christian message.

He then charges Timothy to warn the Ephesians to avoid "quarreling about words." The quarreling had a very negative effect on the Ephesian believers: (1) it accomplished no good purpose, and (2) it worked to the ruin of those who participated in it.

Paul's solution for Timothy is to encourage good conduct. This conduct includes three features:

1. Timothy is to make it his supreme ambition to obtain God's approval.
2. Timothy is to be a workman with no reason to be ashamed.
3. Timothy is to be accurate in developing the truth.

The truth is the gospel. Paul shows concern that Timothy will present the gospel without perverting or distorting it. He is not to be turned aside by disputes about words or mere empty prattle.

Although saddened by the denial of Christian truths by the false teachers, whose teaching would "spread like gangrene," Paul recognizes the durability of the main structures of Christianity. God's solid foundation is unshakable.

An Appeal for Separation (vv. 20–21)

 The "large house" is a metaphor for the church. The church contains both faithful and unfaithful believers. Some serve for desirable ends; others accomplish

"Correctly handle"

This phrase translates a two-word compound from the Greek text ("straight" + "to cut"), with the emphasis on "straight." In reference to handling the Word of Truth, it means to be diligent in its study and to be accurate in its teaching.

"It (the word for "correctly handle") occurs in Prov. 3:6; 11:5 for making straight paths, with which compare Heb. 12:13 and "the Way" in Acts 9:2. Theodoret explains it to mean ploughing a straight furrow. Parry argues that the metaphor is the stone mason cutting the stone straight. Since Paul was a tent-maker and knew how to cut straight the rough camel-hair cloth, why not let that be the metaphor? Certainly plenty of exegesis is crooked enough (crazy-quilt patterns) to call for careful cutting to set it straight" (A. T. Robertson, *WPNT*, IV, pp. 619–20).

53

shameful ends. Paul urges his readers to avoid those who would hinder their good work, namely the false teachers. Paul has three encouraging words about the believer who is an instrument "for noble purposes":

1. Such a person is made holy, set apart for a special purpose before God.

2. Such a person is "useful to the Master." His level of consecration can affect his level of usefulness to God.

3. Such a person is "prepared to do any good work." He will be ready to undertake whatever God calls him to do.

Those who are most useful to God will find they must avoid certain practices, attitudes, and ideas. He urges his readers to make such a separation.

Timothy's Response to Error (vv. 22–26)

The content of Paul's instructions. Paul delivers two imperatives to Timothy: (1) "flee" and (2) "pursue."

1. "Flee the evil desires of youth."

2. "Pursue righteousness, faith, love and peace, along with those who call on the Lord out of a pure heart."

The purpose of Paul's instructions. "In the hope that" signals Paul's two-pronged purpose for his gentle instructions for Timothy:

1. Paul wants the false teachers to experience repentance so they will acknowledge the truth.

2. Paul wants the false teachers to return to sober thinking and win release from Satan's stranglehold.

"But sanctify Christ as Lord in your hearts, always being ready to make a defense to everyone who asks you to give an account for the hope that is in you, yet with gentleness and reverence" (1 Pet. 3:15 NASB).

ℜN

- *Paul warns Timothy to resist the false teachers,*
- *appeals for Timothy to separate from them,*
- *and outlines Timothy's proper response to*
- *them. The best prescription for avoiding entic-*
- *ing errors is a proper presentation of the truth.*
- *Paul urges this on Timothy.*

GUIDING QUESTIONS

1. Paul uses five images from the daily life of his culture. What lessons might we learn from each of these images?

2. What is the point of Paul's trustworthy saying? How might we embrace the truths it teaches?

3. What does Paul mean by "correctly handling" the Word of truth? Cite some examples of failing to correctly handle the Word of truth.

4. Why did Paul appeal to his readers to separate from the false teachers? What is to be Timothy's response to the error of the heretics?

2 TIMOTHY 3 - - - - - - - - - - - - -

THE STUBBORN CHARACTER OF THE FALSE TEACHERS (3:1–9)

In this section, Paul prepares Timothy for the kinds of people he can expect to deal with in his ministry.

What They Are (vv. 1–5)

Paul provides a long list of vices that resemble collections in Rom. 1:29–31 and 1 Tim. 1:9–10.

"Power"

The Greek word is *dunamis*—something that overcomes resistance. C. A. Trentham says, "The power which the New Testament proclaims is the power that brought Christ out of the grave and which enters into every soul committed to Christ . . . Without such power the Christian religion is an empty shell" (C. A. Trenthem *Studies in Timothy*, Convention Press, 1959, p. 123).

In another letter that Paul wrote to Ephesus, he describes what may have been this same phenomenon. "We must become like a mature person— we must grow until we become like Christ and have all His perfection. We will not be tossed about like a ship that the waves carry one way and then another. We will not be influenced by every new teaching we hear from men who are trying to fool us. These men make plans and try any kind of trick to fool people into following the wrong path" (Eph. 4:13b–14 NCV).

Unbridled egotism, greed, disregard for authority, and cruel, callous attitudes toward others are the kinds of things Paul describes here. The presence of people with these vices demonstrate that these were truly hard times.

Paul applies the catalog of vices to the false teachers. He summarizes their behavior with a description that contains these two elements:

1. They maintain a form of godliness;
2. They deny the power of godliness.

For Paul, there was only one solution: stay away from these people.

What They Do (vv. 6–9)

Paul further describes the false teachers. Their methods were most effective among gullible, undisciplined women whose instability resulted from guilt. These woman were constantly learning but never came to know anything.

Paul indicates these teachers opposed the truth with the same level of intensity that the Egyptian magicians, Jannes and Jambres, opposed Moses and Aaron. These teachers' minds were corrupted.

N

- *Paul provides a description of the false teach-*
- *ers. Paul reminds Timothy that this wasn't the*
- *first time God's servants have been opposed by*
- *hypocrites and that such teacher's real motives*
- *will eventually be exposed.*

SOURCES OF STRENGTH FOR ENDURANCE (3:10–17)

Paul uses a frightening picture to portray the opposition Timothy would face. Where could anyone find the strength and wisdom to resist and overcome such opposition? Two sources were Paul's sterling example and the instruction of Scripture.

The Example of Paul (vv. 10–13)

Paul provides a condensed autobiography to draw out lessons from his life for the benefit of his younger disciple. The older apostle's counsel did not come from an "ivory tower" existence. He knew what it was to suffer hardship for the gospel.

Although the enemies of the faith might have seemed victorious for the moment, they would not gain ultimate victory because they were opposed to God. Timothy was not without guidance as he faced the challenge of the false teachers. His guidance consisted of three elements:

1. The truth of the gospel from Paul's teaching and example.
2. His commitment of faith to Jesus Christ, as opposed to new and deceptive teachings.
3. The help of the "holy Scriptures."

The Enrichment of Scripture (vv. 14–17)

Paul reminds Timothy that his inspired source of instruction is the holy Scriptures or literally, the *sacred writings*.

The affirmation of Scripture's inspired nature leads Paul to a discussion of its usefulness. He describes four uses to which Scripture can be put:

Teaching. Scripture is a positive source of Christian doctrine. Out of the twenty-one times the term *teaching* appears in the New Testament, Paul uses it fifteen times in the Pastoral Epistles.

"Every Scripture is God-breathed"

"In contrast with the teaching of imposters, The Christian faith rests securely on its inspired Scriptures, which have been carefully preserved from generation to generation. Therefore, Paul calls Timothy to remember that "all scripture is given by inspiration of God,' or is 'God-breathed.' The Scriptures are the result of God's personal intervention on the plane of human history and of his personal encounter through the Spirit with his people and prophets. "Revelation" means God's presence in the events of history. "Inspiration" means his presence in the recording of those events" (C. A. Trentham in *Studies in Timothy*, p. 128).

Because of the prominence of heresy among his readers, Paul emphasizes sound doctrine.

Rebuking. This may refer to a rebuke that exposes the errors of false teachers. It may also refer to reproof in our personal lives. Scripture can show sinners their failures, clarify the point or doctrine, and lead them to a new sense of peace and wholeness.

> "Reproof was especially important in Judaism, where it had to be done privately and gently first."
> Craig S. Keener in *IVP Bible Background Commentary*, p. 630

Correcting. Scripture is helpful for convicting the misguided and disobedient of their errors and restoring them to the right paths.

Moral training. This is training that leads to righteous living. In Eph. 6:4, the term for "training" (the same term used in 2 Tim 3:16) denotes a system of discipline used by a parent to develop Christian character in a child. Here it describes a system of discipline in Scripture that leads to a holy lifestyle.

The reason for using Scripture in these ways is "so that the man of God may be thoroughly equipped for every good work." For Timothy, this meant that he was furnished completely to do whatever God called him to perform. What a tragedy for any Christian to be labeled spiritually unprepared for a task when the means of preparation are readily at hand!

Paul teaches Timothy several lessons in these verses that are applicable to us today. Christians receive strength for their pilgrimage from two sources—the lives of other believers and the instruction of God's Word.

GUIDING QUESTIONS

1. Describe the character of the false teachers. What two principles for our consideration emerge from Paul's description of these heretics?

2. Who were the victims of these false teachers? Why were they able to subvert their victims?

3. What does "God-breathed" mean? Why is the inspiration of Scripture such an important Christian doctrine?

2 TIMOTHY 4

A CHARGE FOR CONSISTENT BEHAVIOR (4:1–5)

In this section, Paul continues the appeal for doctrinal soundness, which he began in 2:14. He underscores Timothy's role in thwarting the advance of heresy in Ephesus. The intensity of Paul's feeling is evident from his use of nine imperatives in this part of his letter.

Context of the Charge (v. 1)

Paul makes this solemn charge to Timothy not just as man to man but in the very presence of God the Father and Jesus Christ, who will serve as judge of both the living and the dead.

Charge to Ministry (v. 2)

Paul's charge to Timothy is to "preach the Word." He then follows this charge with four commands that indicate how Timothy is to carry out his charge:

1. Timothy is to stand "prepared in season and out of season." This means he must

"Be Prepared"

A.T. Robertson gives these translations of this Greek term: "Take a stand," "carry on," "stick to it."

always be "on duty" and take advantage of every opportunity for service.

2. Timothy is to correct error by the use of reasoned judgment.

3. Timothy is to give hope to the faint-hearted by providing tender encouragement in the face of discouraging opposition.

4. Timothy is to obey with "great patience and careful instruction."

Reason for the Charge (vv. 3–4)

Paul gives a stern charge to Timothy to declare the truth because he foresees Christendom increasing its appetite for error rather than truth. Only sturdy pastors are able to endure such unstable congregations. Paul sees three developments that emphasize the need for countering error:

1. Listeners would no longer "put up with sound doctrine." They would find the content and demands of the gospel unpalatable.

2. They would raise up teachers "to suit their own desires."

3. They will do all this to satisfy the "itching" in their ears.

It is important to note that Paul is warning professing believers in this passage.

Timothy's Personal Charge (v. 5)

What should be the stance of the pastor who sees these developments? He is to remain poised ("keep your head") and suffer any hardship that results from his faithfulness to his charge. Timothy is to continue his work by spreading the gospel and discharging his ministerial duties.

■ *Indifference from listeners must not be per-*
■ *mitted to shut off the proclamation of the*
■ *gospel by believers. Timothy is to remain*
■ *alert and watchful of opposition while endur-*
■ *ing all necessary afflictions in spreading the*
■ *gospel. There is encouragement. Christians*
■ *committed to declaring God's message to*
■ *indifferent audiences can expect God's*
■ *strength, power, and ultimate blessing.*

THE REWARD FOR SELF-SACRIFICE (4:6–8)

Paul now speaks of the expectation of his approaching death. Here he outlines the sacrifice he has made, the service he has rendered, and the reward he anticipates.

The Sacrifice of Life (v. 6)

In these verses Paul shares his own attitude and faith in the face of his impending execution. His statements may have been dictated just days or hours before his death. Here we can see how one great Christian viewed the possibility of sacrificing his own life for the sake of the gospel.

He uses sacrifical imagery to portray his own death. First, he compares the pouring out of his energy in ministry to the pouring out of the wine of an Old Testament drink offering. Second, he describes his death as a "departure" of a ship by the lifting its anchor and the breaking up of a camp of soldiers. Both the ship and the soldiers were going home.

By faith Paul gives a marvelous appraisal of the grim prospects of his death. Timothy may have read the story of this buoyant faith through a covering of tears.

"Paul had had his preliminary hearing before Nero, and was expecting the final one, and death. He knew it would not be crucifixion, for a citizen of the Roman Empire was not crucified. If the death penalty was demanded by the State, it would be decapitation, hence the figurative reference to a libation" (*The Pastoral Epistles in the Greek New Testament*, by Kenneth S. Wuest, p. 160).

The Service of Ministry (v. 7)

But Paul has no regrets as he nears the end. He uses three metaphors to reflect the struggle of his ministry:

"I have fought the good fight." Paul had done his best in the contest.

"I have finished the race." He had faithfully followed the course laid out by his Lord.

"I have kept the faith." This may have involved either maintaining the sound doctrine of Christianity intact or by keeping loyalty to the trust that the Father had given him.

With these words Paul is not boasting of his accomplishments but reflecting on the cause of his life with a statement of confidence. He is describing what the grace of God has produced in him.

The Reward of Obedience (v. 8)

When a runner in an athletic contest of the first century crossed the finish line as the victor, he was assured of receiving the emblem of victory. Paul is also sure he will receive a victor's crown: a "crown of righteousness." This may refer to a reward for righteous behavior or a gift consisting of righteousness awarded by the Judge when He returns.

$\mathcal{N}$

■ *The knowledge that God rewards and recog-*
■ *nizes faithful Christian service is an incen-*
■ *tive to godly living. God is faithful to*
■ *believers; He will not ignore their works but*
■ *will justly evaluate all of them.*

A FEW REQUESTS AND WARNINGS (4:9–15)

"Bring the cloak"

As Paul wrote these verses, he seems to have been convinced of the nearness of his death. There may have been some possibility, however, of a further delay in the execution of the sentence imposed on him. He urges Timothy, therefore, to come to him soon.

The apostle asks Timothy to bring his cloak along with his books and parchments. There has been much speculation about the nature of these books and parchments. It's possible that nothing was written on them. Perhaps they were simply writing materials for Paul's use.

Paul makes special mention of a coppersmith named Alexander. He warned Timothy about this man as the fellow had vigorously resisted Paul. Timothy was to be on his guard for him.

"Paul also wanted his cloak, which probably was a heavy wool garment, to protect him from the winter. It was getting cold in Rome. The cold, wintry winds would pass through the subterranean corridors of the Mamertine Prison, chilling the bones of the aged apostle to the very marrow. This was the only cloak Paul had. Those who seem to feel that the Christian gospel promises an abundance of material comforts to all followers to Christ need to remember that Paul was so poor that he could not afford to lose an old cloak at Troas. We know nothing about Carpus save that he was the custodian of the cloak of Paul" (C. A. Trentham, *Studies in Timothy*, pp. 138–139).

A REMINDER OF GOD'S DELIVERING POWER (4:16–18)

Paul gives Timothy fresh information about his lack of support from Christian friends and the magnificent strength the Lord had supplied. The memory of divine protection leads Paul to an outburst of praise.

"The Lord stood at my side and gave me strength." In contrast to the desertion of friends, the Lord stood beside Paul to provide strength. Two results developed from the help and strength God provided in the trial:

1. *The gospel was fully proclaimed so the heathen heard it.* God gave Paul the courage and opportunity to preach. By doing so, Paul fulfilled his plans of reaching Rome with the gospel.

2. *Paul's deliverance from the "lion's mouth."* Interpreters have identified the lion as one of these three: the literal lions of the amphitheater, the emperor Nero, or Satan.

- *Paul had been deserted by friends and*
- *wronged by others. In the midst of difficult*
- *circumstances and approaching death, Paul*
- *gave testimony to God's faithfulness. He was*
- *totally confident that God was in control of*
- *his life. As Christians we, too, must learn to*
- *rejoice in divine victory and avoid succumb-*
- *ing to disappointments in a spirit of vindic-*
- *tiveness.*

CONCLUSION (4:19–21)

As was customary in letters of the first century, Paul concludes his letter with personal greetings. These include Priscilla and Aquila, Onesiphorus, and Trophimus. Paul makes a final request to Timothy to visit him "before winter" so there would not be an additional delay.

Paul first met Aquila and Priscilla in Corinth (Acts 18:2). His relationship with them had remained strong and a source of comfort over many years of ministry.

BENEDICTION (4:22)

In the benediction, Paul expresses a personal word for Timothy. He wishes that God might strengthen Timothy personally so the younger leader might faithfully discharge his task. These are likely the last written words of Paul.

GUIDING QUESTIONS

1. Upon what realities did Paul base his charge to Timothy? How do we relate today to these realities in our ministries?
2. Specifically, what was Paul's charge to Timothy? Why was it so important that Timothy follow through?

3. Describe Paul's attitude toward his approaching death. What are your thoughts about death?

4. Why is it so important to preach the Word?

TITUS 1

SALUTATION (1:1–4)

Author (vv. 1–3)

In his letters to churches or individuals, Paul uses the form of introductory greeting customary in first-century letter writing. In this epistle to Titus, Paul identifies himself as the source of the letter and Titus as the recipient, followed by his stated desire for God's blessing upon Titus.

Paul typically includes several self-descriptions to establish his authority and right to speak. He does this by identifying himself as "a servant of God and an apostle of Jesus Christ." The term *apostle* means "one who is sent." Paul classifies himself among those earlier apostles, such as Peter, James, and John, who had been called and commissioned directly by the risen Lord.

The goal of Paul's apostolic ministry was the "hope of eternal life." The "word" Paul preached is the message of God's redemptive deed in the death and Resurrection of Jesus Christ. This was the message Paul proclaimed in obedience to the trust God had placed in him by calling him as an apostle.

Recipient (v. 4a)

Titus is the recipient of the letter. He was one of Paul's closest missionary associates. Paul calls Titus his "true son." In common usage, this phrase means natural, as opposed to an adopted or foster child. This father-son relationship, however, is understood in the context of the community of faith. Perhaps Paul had won Titus to Christ.

Paul's greeting is standard. "Grace," God's unmerited love, is the basis of our relationship with Him. "Peace" is the new relationship we enjoy with God and His people because of His grace. We have been reconciled to God and to one another.

THE CHARGE TO APPOINT ELDERS ON CRETE (1:5)

Paul now turns his attention to Titus's immediate task with the churches at Crete. There was work yet to be accomplished in Crete, and Paul instructs Titus to complete the work that had been started there. He gives Titus a primary directive, which is to "appoint elders in every town." This meant he was to appoint elders in every Cretan town where a Christian congregation was located.

THE QUALIFICATIONS FOR ELDERS ON CRETE (1:6–9)

The qualifications presented require acceptable conditions in three basic areas of the prospective elder's life, namely:

1. His marriage and family,
2. His personality and character traits, and
3. His devotion to God's Word and his commitment to teaching and preaching the true gospel message.

Marriage and Family Qualifications (v. 6)

Two aspects of the prospective elder's family life are noted: his marriage and the faith and conduct of his children.

"The husband of one wife." These simple words have proven difficult to understand, and the

Crete

Crete is a long, narrow mountainous island (175 miles long, 35 miles at its widest point) south of mainland Greece. Crete was the center of the Minoan maritime empire named after the legendary King Minos. This brilliant civilization fell suddenly, perhaps by an earthquake followed by conquest, about 1400 B.C., leaving written tablets in the oldest known scripts of Europe.

By the second century B.C., Crete had a substantial Jewish population, powerful enough to obtain the protection of Rome. The large and influential Jewish population on Crete, as well as the initial exposure of Cretan Jews to the gospel at Pentecost, suggests that Crete was a fertile location for missionary work.

The character of the people is described in a quotation from a prophet of their own: "Cretans are always liars, evil brutes, lazy gluttons" (Titus 1:12), words attributed to the Cretan seer Epimenides, who was also credited with having advised the Athenians to set up altars to unknown gods (cf. Acts 17:23).

"Elder"

The term *elder* simply means "an aged man." However, in the context of New Testament church organization, elder is a technical term signifying a church leader. It is likely that this term was carried over from the synagogue, which probably served as a limited model for early church organization.

interpretations derived from them are many and varied. A basic question concerning this qualification is whether the elder is restricted to *one* marriage to *one* woman in his lifetime. Obviously, this phrase would eliminate a bigamist or polygamist from consideration. Since the Scriptures do not prohibit remarriage after the death of a spouse, and actually encourage it in some cases, it is unlikely that such a remarried man should be disqualified.

While it was not Paul's intention to prohibit unmarried men from becoming elders, it may be assumed that the majority of candidates would be married and that Paul may have preferred married men to hold these positions because of their experience in leading the family unit.

"Whose children believe." The second aspect of the prospective elder's family life concerns his children, specifically their faith and personal conduct. This passage and 1 Tim. 3:4 are similar in that they both require that children be well-behaved and obedient. However, the addition of "whose children believe" in Titus makes this condition even more stringent. This additional requirement that the elder is capable of influencing his own children to become Christians demonstrates Paul's conviction that effective spiritual leadership in the home suggests that same probability of effective leadership in the church.

Personality and Character Qualifications (vv. 7–8)

Paul provides a succinct list of five negative and six positive personality and character traits of the prospective elder. The following chart lists these and adds their extended meanings:

Personality and Character Qualifications of Elders

TRAIT	EXTENDED MEANING
NEGATIVE ("NOT"):	
Not overbearing	Flexible in his own opinions; considerate of other viewpoints
Not quick-tempered	Controls his emotions and exercises proper judgment
Not given to drunkenness	Is not given to much wine; considerate of weaker brothers in this area
Not violent	Not given to physical (or verbal) violence
Not pursuing dishonest gain	Absolutely honest in money matters; does not use his Christian service as an opportunity for financial profit
POSITIVE:	
Hospitable	Devoted to the welfare of others
Loves good	Includes good things as well as good men
Self-controlled	Mastery of his mind, emotions, words, and deeds
Upright	Committed to doing what is right; to a life of devotion and service to God
Holy	Separated to devotion and service of God
Disciplined	Exhibits the power of lordship over oneself

Devotion to Sound Doctrine (v. 9)

The elder "must hold firmly" to orthodox biblical teaching. Two basic functions of the elder's role in the church emanate from his own personal devotion to the truth of God's Word:

1. *To encourage others.* Here, within the context of the elder's function toward believers, "to encourage others by sound

doctrine" indicates comfort and edification in "the trustworthy message."

2. *To refute those who oppose sound doctrine.* The goal of the refutation of false teaching is not to destroy the opponent but rather to restore him to "sound doctrine." Such a situation would also require that the elder be courageous in his willingness to confront a so-called Christian brother.

N

■ *Paul presents qualifications for church lead-*
■ *ers. Elder candidates must meet certain stan-*
■ *dards with regard to home life, personality*
■ *and character traits, and doctrinal integrity.*

THE NEED FOR QUALIFIED CHURCH LEADERSHIP (1:10–16)

The problem confronting the churches in Crete was serious. They were being disrupted by false teachers. The impact of these false teachers was considerable; they were "ruining whole households." Paul feels that they are exploiting the churches for "the sake of dishonest gain," and believes that they "must be silenced." Paul's response to their rebelliousness and false teaching is to command Titus to "rebuke" them.

Paul provides two descriptions of their false teachings:

"Jewish myths." The myths Paul refers to possibly were concerned with Jewish and Gnostic ideas combined in Hellenistic Judaism and transferred to Christianity by Jewish-Christian converts.

"The commands of those who reject the truth." This description recalls Isa. 29:13: "These people come near to me with their mouth and honor

me with their lips, but their hearts are far from me. Their worship of me is made up only of rules taught by men" (the Septuagint, the Greek translation of the Old Testament). Jesus quoted this very passage to the Pharisees when they disputed Him concerning religious ceremony and the matter of being clean or unclean. Those persons who tenaciously hold to these human commandments or tradition (that is, religious rituals that have no real meaning) are "those who reject the truth," according to Paul (1:14), or who "have let go of the commands of God," according to Jesus (Mark 7:8).

"I am in the Lord Jesus, and I know that there is no food that is wrong to eat. But if a person believes that something is wrong, then that thing is wrong for him" (Rom. 14:14 NCV).

Titus 1:14–16 should be studied in light of Jesus' teaching in Mark 7:1–23 and its parallel passage in Matt. 15:1–20.

■ Paul attempts to expose and rebuke the false
■ teachers who were endangering the Cretan
■ churches. He uses strong language as he
■ exposes their error of adding external reli-
■ gious requirements to the gospel of God's
■ grace. Because of the serious perversion of
■ the doctrine of salvation, it is evident how
■ much the churches of Crete needed strong,
■ qualified leaders.

GUIDING QUESTIONS

1. Who was Titus? What was his mission?

2. What qualifications did Paul lay down for prospective elders?

3. What is proper interpretation of the requirement: "husband of one wife"? How does a church apply this requirement to a man who has remarried? To one who has divorced?

4. How can we avoid the trap of legalistic Christianity and other false teachings?

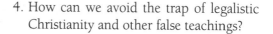

TITUS 2

EXHORTATIONS FOR THE RIGHT BEHAVIOR (2:1–10)

Having addressed Titus's duties with regard to church organizational leadership and the confrontation of false teaching, Paul encourages Titus to exhort various groups within the church to meet certain standards of behavior. Five specific groups are to receive specific exhortations: the older men (v. 2), the older women (v. 3), the young women (vv. 4–5), the young men (vv. 6–8), and slaves (vv. 9–10). These groups, designated by age, sex, and social position, would certainly include each believer and church member on Crete.

Especially noteworthy is the occurrence of the phrase "so that" (three times, vv. 5, 8, 10). Each occurrence begins a clause that expresses the goal or purpose of the behavior that is encouraged. Furthermore, these clauses indicate that proper Christian behavior has a significant impact on pagan attitudes toward Christianity (v. 5), silencing opponents by correct Christian teaching (v. 8), and attracting a lost world to Christianity (v. 10), thus affecting the entire missionary enterprise of the church..

In contrast to the opponents in 1:10–16, who taught error that resulted in their being "unfit for doing anything good" (v. 16), Paul emphasizes in 2:1–10 that good works are a necessary and natural result of believing "sound doctrine." To be rescued from sin and death through faith in Jesus Christ must result in a changed life that displays self-control and reflects God's love and grace.

Behavior in Accord with Sound Doctrine (v. 1)

Paul begins with a sharp command for Titus. His message to Titus is "teach what is in accord with sound doctrine." He asserts Titus's personal responsibility for instructing the Cretan believers regarding their own appropriate Christian behavior and responsibilities.

Exhortation for Older Men (v. 2)

This group may have been men of an age sufficient to have raised a family and seen their children begin families of their own. Titus was to exhort or encourage these older men to be:

1. *Temperate*—possessing complete clarity of mind and its resulting good judgment.
2. *Worthy of respect*—with dignity; not frivolous or silly.
3. *Self-controlled*—behaving sensibly.
4. *Sound*—doctrinally healthy.

Furthermore, the older men are to be sound in these three areas:

Faith. This is trust in God, manifested in loyal Christian living.

Love. This is commitment to the welfare of others without regard for merit.

Endurance. This is a triumphant stance in the face of persecution and difficulties.

The Older Women (v. 3)

As children grow up and leave home, the older woman's focus may become less defined as her familial responsibilities become less demanding. This may contribute to feelings of uselessness, loneliness, low self-esteem, and self-pity.

"Self-control"

The way modern translators render this word indicates a sober, temperate, calm, and dispassionate approach to life, having mastered personal desires and passions. Biblical admonitions expect God's people to exercise self-control (Prov. 25:28; 1 Cor. 7:5; 1 Thess. 5:6; 1 Tim. 3:2; 2 Tim. 3:3; Gal. 5:23; 2 Tim. 1:7; 2 Pet. 1:6).

Freedom in Christ does not give believers liberty to cast off all moral restraint as some members in Galatia and other churches apparently believed. Nor does it call for a withdrawal from life and its temptations. It calls for a self-disciplined life following Christ's example of being in the world but not of the world.

Paul repeatedly uses the term "self-control" throughout this passage in Titus and applies it to all the groups he addresses. This indicates the need for Christians to live sensibly and reasonably within a fragmented world characterized by chaos and confusion.

"Be subject to"

This phrase is an instruction regarding the relationship between husband and wife (cf. Eph. 5:24; Col. 3:18; 1 Pet. 3:1, 5). The term is also used in a variety of other contexts, including, for example, the subjection of all things to Christ, the subjection of persons to civil authorities, the subjection of slaves to masters, and the subjection of one Christian to another. In his *The Epistle to the Romans,* C. E. B. Cranfield, speaking of this subjection, states, "It is the responsible acceptance of a relationship in which God has placed one and the resulting honest attempt to fulfill the duties which it imposes on one" (p. 662).

Paul suggests in this passage that older women should possess personal godliness, be worthy of respect, and play an essential role in the lives of the young women in the church. The concept of spiritual mentoring is evident in this passage.

Titus is to encourage the older women with the following exhortations.

1. *Be reverent*—a way of life appropriate to a priestess serving in God's temple. The phrase "in the way they live" indicates the outward expression of an inner character.
2. *Not being slanderers*—avoiding lies, false accusations, and malicious gossip.
3. *Not addicted to much wine*—control over physical appetites.
4. *Teach what is good*—advising the young women.

The Younger Women (vv. 4–5)

The young women are to "love their husbands and children." Because Paul expresses this first, it may suggest the high value Paul gave to the congenial and cohesive Christian family unit.

Communicating Paul's exhortations for the younger women was not Titus's direct responsibility. Rather, this was to be the duty of the older women. Of the desirable qualities for Christian young women, several presuppose a life involving marriage and family:

- "To love their husbands and children"
- "Self-controlled and pure"
- "To be busy at home"
- "To be kind"
- "To be subject to their husbands"

It must also be noted that to "to be subject to" does not imply a position of inferiority of being. As a general rule, all Christian doctrinal discussion concerning relationships between men and women should begin with Paul's statement in Gal. 3:28 that "there is . . . neither male nor female . . . in Christ."

The Younger Men (vv. 7–8)

Paul's exhortation for the younger men is to be conveyed by Titus's words and personal example. Titus is to encourage them toward these qualities:

1. To achieve self-control—self-mastery and sensibleness
2. To set an "example by doing what is good"—to be a role model of good works, in contrast to the false teachers
3. To show integrity in their teaching—the art of effectively communicating the true gospel message
4. To demonstrate seriousness—characterized by dignity and what will inspire respect from hearers
5. To demonstrate soundness of speech—healthy, well-thought-out presentations of the Christian gospel.

Paul's stated goal for exhorting these qualities in younger men is "so that those who oppose you may be ashamed because they have nothing bad to say about us." Hostile critics will ultimately be ashamed in the sense of publicly suffering loss of respect as it becomes apparent that their criticisms are groundless.

Instructions for Slaves (vv. 9–10)

The institution of slavery is indefensible from the Christian point of view. Paul expresses his belief that the division between slave and free belonged to the old order that was under the judgment of God. In Christ's church, which belonged to the new order, there is "neither . . . slave nor free" (Gal. 3:28).

Under the conditions of the ancient world, the only advice the apostle could give to believing slaves was to be Christian in their slavery. Their Christian character could be demonstrated through obedience, honesty, and faithfulness. Paul exhorts Titus to encourage these qualities in slaves:

- "To be subject to their masters in everything."
- "To try to please" their masters.
- "Not to talk back" to their masters.
- "Not steal from" their masters.
- Show trustworthiness.
- Make attractive the teaching about God and Jesus in every way.

"Grace"

Kenneth Wuest points out that the Greeks used *charis* (grace) to refer to a favor that one does for another person, expecting no return. But, these favors were always done for friends. Christ gave *grace* a far richer meaning because the favor He did at Calvary was done not for friends but for those who hated him. Paul reminds the Romans that while we were still His enemies, He provided a way of reconciliation to God through his death (Rom. 5:10).

■ *Paul's specific exhortations to the various*
■ *groups within the Cretan church in 2:1–10*
■ *reveal two foundational aspects of Christian*
■ *behavior. First, his repeated use of the term*
■ *"self-control" throughout this passage is*
■ *applicable to all groups. Second, the repeated*
■ *use of the phrase "so that" (indicating pur-*
■ *pose) demonstrates the missionary aspects of*
■ *everyday Christian behavior within a hostile*
■ *and lost world.*

The Doctrinal Basis for Christian Behavior (2:11–15)

The material in this section is highly compressed but incredibly rich.

The Truths of God's Grace (v. 11)

Paul uses the connecting word *for* to link what follows with what has gone before. What he says, in effect, is, to take on this new life-style—whatever your station in life, *for* or *because* God's grace has appeared.

A person who sees, understands, and accepts this grace can't easily go back to his or her former lifestyle.

God's Grace as a Teacher (vv. 12–15)

God's grace educates us in Christian behavior. The force of the verb *teaches* is that of present tense, continuous action.

1. *God's grace teaches us to say "no" to godless-ness.* This refers to a conscious, willful repudiation of thoughts, words, and actions that are opposed to true godli-ness.
2. *God's grace teaches us to "live self-controlled, upright, and godly lives."* Self-control involves being sensible and sober-minded. *Upright* denotes conduct that cannot be condemned. *Godly* denotes lives that are pleasing to God.

Through Jesus' work of redemption, God brought into being a people who are His price-less possession. Immorality is inconsistent with this status conferred upon us by God. In view of this special relation with God, believers are to take their moral and ethical lives seriously. We are to be "eager to do what is good."

"Teaches us"

The Greek verb translated "teach" means "to instruct, educate." However, its biblical usage may contain the nuance of discipline or chastisement. Education in Christian behavior is seldom a painless process as it involves the correction of human behavior that by nature stands in opposition to God. Paul states the aspects of this education both negatively and positively.

■ *The highest and purest motivation for Chris-*
■ *tian behavior is not based on what we can do*
■ *for God, but upon what God has done for us*
■ *and will yet do. The false teachers on Crete*
■ *assumed their religious works earned them*
■ *God's favor. Apostle Paul teaches that only*

- *as we grasp the significance of God's grace*
- *can we eagerly do what is pleasing to Him.*

GUIDING QUESTIONS

1. Describe Paul's concept of "self-control." Why does he give it such high priority?
2. What instructions does Paul provide for the older men? The younger men?
3. What instructions does Paul provide for the older women? The younger women?
4. In the New Testament, what does it mean for a wife to be subject her husband?
5. How does the grace of God "teach" us? What does it teach us?

TITUS 3

THE NEED FOR CHRISTIAN BEHAVIORAL STANDARDS (3:1–2)

Paul takes up the matter of standards of Christian conduct with regard to pagan society in general. His exhortations in 2:1–10 appear to relate more directly to Christian behavior among believers and the impact that such behavior has on the unbeliever. Here Paul addresses the direct relationship the Cretan Christians had with the pagan world.

Respect for Governmental Authorities (v. 1)

Paul takes a positive attitude toward the government, as is also true of Peter (1 Pet. 2:13–14). When the Pastoral Epistles were written, the government was viewed as beneficent rather than a hindrance to the gospel. According to this passage, the duty of the believer in civic matters is threefold:

1. Be submissive;
2. Be obedient;
3. Be honest.

This exhortation extends the Christian's responsibilities from a passive posture (obeying laws) to an active, positive involvement in society.

This idea is a practical outworking of Jesus' teaching about being "the salt of the earth . . . and the light of the world...that they may see your good deeds and praise your father in heaven" (Matt. 5:13–16).

Respect for All (v. 2)

The question of how Christians are to relate to their pagan neighbors was especially difficult in the early days of Christianity. Church members, a minority of the population, were often objects of pagan and Jewish hostility and slander.

According to Paul's instructions, the relation of believers to non-Christians is to be governed by the principles of love. Their conversation with their unbelieving contemporaries should be loving, gentle, and courteous.

■ *In this section Paul takes up the matter of*
■ *standards of Christian conduct with regard*
■ *to pagan society in general. This conduct*
■ *includes believers' respect for governmental*
■ *authorities and maintaining civic responsi-*
■ *bilities. It also requires that they be governed*
■ *by the principles of love in their relationship*
■ *to non-Christians in a pagan society.*

THE THEOLOGICAL BASIS FOR PROPER BEHAVIOR (3:3–8)

In this section, Paul describes the degenerate conditions of the pagan society in which Christians had to live. Interestingly, his comments focus on the human condition within society. Paul identifies himself and all Christians with sinful and degenerate humanity. Christians, though at one time degenerate and lost, are objects of God's kindness and love, which results in their salvation. Christians are to demonstrate this same kindness and love toward lost individuals and society, making Christianity attractive and resulting in the salvation of others.

Verses 4–7 eloquently summarize God's work in humanity's salvation. Paul presents several key doctrinal ideas.

"The kindness and love of God . . . appeared." God's kindness includes His generosity and goodness, especially toward humanity and for humanity's benefit. God's love speaks of His love for humankind. The purpose of God's kindness and love is to bring salvation.

"He saved us." Salvation is not through humankind's attempts to achieve salvation through its own efforts. It comes as a result of God's mercy.

"Because of his mercy." Salvation depends solely and completely on God's grace, displayed in "his mercy," revealed and achieved by His Son, Jesus Christ, and applied to humankind by the Holy Spirit.

"This is a trustworthy saying"

This phrase is used in all three of the Pastoral Epistles (1 Tim. 1:5; 3:1; 4:9; 2 Tim. 2:11; Titus 3:8). It serves to emphasize either what is to be said or what has been said and may indicate Paul's intentional use of creeds, catechisms, hymns, or liturgical material. The "trustworthy saying" in this passage probably includes verses 4–7.

- *Paul describes the degenerate condition of*
- *the pagan society in which Christians had to*
- *live. Christians are to demonstrate kindness*
- *and love to lost individuals and society, mak-*
- *ing Christianity attractive and resulting in*
- *the salvation of others.*

PAUL'S FINAL WARNING CONCERNING FALSE TEACHING AND DIVISION (3:9–11)

Having offered an eloquent doctrinal summary of the gospel and its motivation to profitable good works, Paul again warns Titus about the "unprofitable" works of the false teachers.

Paul's Warnings About False Teachings in the Pastoral Epistles

PASSAGE	TOPIC
1 Tim. 1:4	genealogies
1 Tim. 6:4	controversies and quarrels
2 Tim. 2:16	threat of heresy
2 Tim.2:23	foolish and stupid arguments.

These occurrences suggest that similar if not identical false doctrines were common during this period of church history.

Paul describes a false teacher as a "divisive person." Concerning those persons who promote false teaching, Paul commands that Titus "warn a divisive person once, and then warn him a second time. After that, have nothing to do with him" (v. 10).

Division can be destructive. Divisions within the church result in believers who are confused, frustrated, angry, and hurt. They become ineffective in ministering to one another and to a lost world in desperate need of the gospel of Jesus Christ.

Paul concludes by saying, "You may be sure that such a man is warped and sinful; he is self-condemned." We can be sure about these three things about a divisive person.

1. *He is "warped."* The force of the verb Paul uses here means that this person has been and remains off track.

2. *He is "sinful."* This is a present-tense verb, meaning that he willfully *continues* to sin.

This process is similar to what Jesus commands: "And if your brother sins, go and reprove him in private; if he listens to you, you have won your brother. But if he does not listen to you, take one or two more with you, so that by the mouth of two or three witnesses every fact may be confirmed. And if he refuses to listen to them, tell it to the church; and if he refuses to listen even to the church, let him be to you as a Gentile and a tax-gatherer" (Matt. 18:15:17 NASB).

He has been perverted and persists in his sinful way.

3. *He is "self-condemned."* He refuses to heed the counsel of those who are trying to win him from his erring ways. This refusal amounts to his own condemnation of himself.

- *Paul closes his instruction to Titus by reem-*
- *phasizing the significance of refuting false*
- *teaching. The goal of false teachers is to deny*
- *a true knowledge of God and destroy the doc-*
- *trinal unity of the church. When the church*
- *cannot agree on the essentials of Christianity*
- *and is characterized by conflict and divi-*
- *sions, it is ineffective in a lost world as well*
- *as displeasing to God.*

CONCLUDING REMARKS (3:12–15)

Paul ends this letter with personal directions, comments, and greetings.

Personal Directions (vv. 12–14)

When either Artemas or Tychicus was sent to Crete, Titus is to make an effort to rejoin Paul. Artemas is not mentioned elsewhere. Tychicus was the bearer of the Epistle to the Colossians. Paul plans to send one of them to take the place of Titus so he will be free to leave his responsibility in their hands.

Titus is to do all he can to provide for Zenas and Apollos in their journey. Supplying the needs of traveling missionaries as they departed so they would not suffer from lack of food on their journey was an honored expectation among early Christians.

"Paul is going to replace Titus on Crete with someone and therefore urges him to join him in doing ministry in Nicopolis (v. 12)."
George W. Knight III in *Evangelical Commentary on the Bible* (Grand Rapids: Baker), p. 118

Closing Salutations (v. 15)

The close of this letter is in keeping with the practice of letter writing of the day. The final greeting is typically Pauline. From his point of view, the Christian life is a matter of grace from beginning to end. We are saved by grace and sustained by grace, and we enter into our inheritance by grace.

"Grace be with you all" is a prayer for God's grace to be realized in each believer's life. "You all" suggests that although this letter is designated for Titus, Paul expects it to be shared with the entire Cretan church. Paul could ask no higher blessing on Titus and his charges than that they continue to receive the grace of God.

- Paul closes the letter by commending Titus
- and the Cretan believers to the grace of God.

GUIDING QUESTIONS

1. What is the believer's proper attitude toward civic responsibilities?
2. What should govern the relationship of believers to non-Christians?
3. Discuss the doctrinal basis for Christian behavior. What are the key concepts involved?
4. What are the three "sure things" about a divisive person?

The following list is a collection of the sources and reference works used for this volume. All are from Broadman & Holman's list of reference resources. They should accommodate the reader's need for more specific information by offering an expanded treatment of the Pastoral Epistles. All of these works will greatly aid in the reader's study, teaching, and presentation of the Pastoral Epistles. The accompanying annotations can be helpful in guiding the reader to the proper resources.

Adams, J. McKee, Rev. By Joseph A. Callaway, *Biblical Backgrounds*. This work provides valuable information on the physical and geographical settings of the New Testament. Its many color maps and other features add depth and understanding.

Blair, Joe, *Introducing the New Testament*, pp. 177–84. Designed as a core text for New Testament survey courses, this volume helps the reader understand the content and principles of the New Testament. Its features include many maps and photos, outlines, and discussion questions.

Cate, Robert L., *A History of the New Testament and Its Time*. An excellent and thorough survey of the birth and growth of the Christian faith in the first-century world.

Holman Bible Dictionary. An exhaustive, alphabetically arranged resource of Bible-related subjects. An excellent tool of definitions and other information on the people, places, things, and events of the Bible.

Holman Bible Handbook, pp. 736–43. A comprehensive treatment that offers outlines, commentary on key themes and sections, and full-color photos, illustrations, charts, and maps. Provides an emphasis on the broader theological teachings.

Lea, Thomas D. and Hayne P. Griffin Jr., *1, 2 Timothy, Titus* (The New American Commentary), vol . 34.

Lea, Thomas D., *The New Testament: Its Background and Message*, pp. 469–99. An excellent resource for background material—political, cultural, historical, and religious. Provides background information in broad strokes on specific books, including the Gospels. Includes a scholarly treatment of the text of the Pastoral Epistles that provides emphases on the text itself, background, and theological considerations.

McQuay, Earl P., *Keys to Interpreting the Bible.* This work provides a fine introduction to the study of the Bible that is invaluable for home Bible studies, lay members of a local church, or students.

McQuay, Earl P., *Learning to Study the Bible.* This study guide presents a helpful procedure that uses the principles basic to effective and thorough Bible study. Using Philippians as a model, the various methods of Bible study are applied. Excellent for home Bible studies, lay members of a local church, and students.

Robertson, A. T., *A Grammar of the Greek New Testament in the Light of Historical Research.* An exhaustive, scholarly work on the underlying language of the New Testament. Provides advanced insights into the grammatical, syntactical, and lexical aspects of the New Testament.

Robertson, A. T., *Word Pictures in the New Testament*, "The Epistles of Paul," vol. 4, pp. 559–634. This six-volume series provides insights into the language of the Greek New Testament. Provides word studies as well as grammatical and background insights into the Pastoral Epistles.

Tolbert, Malcolm O., *Philippians, Colossians, 1 & 2 Thessalonians, 1 & 2 Timothy, Titus, Philemon* (Layman's Bible Book Commentary), pp. 97–163. A popular-level treatment of the Pastoral Epistles, this easy-to-use volume provides a relevant and practical perspective for the reader.